SATIE SEEN THROUGH HIS LETTERS

ORNELLA VOLTA

SATIE SEEN THROUGH HIS LETTERS

translated by
Michael Bullock

introduced by
John Cage

Marion Boyars
London · New York

Published in Great Britain and the United States in 1989 by
Marion Boyars Publishers
24 Lacy Road, London SW15 1NL and
26 East 33rd Street, New York, N.Y. 10016

Distributed in Australia by Wild and Woolley, Glebe, N.S.W.

British Library Cataloguing in Publication Data

Satie, Erik
    Satie seen through his letters.
    1. Satie — Erik   2. Composers — France
    —Biography
    I. Title   II. Volta, Ornella
    780'.924   ML410.S196

Library of Congress Cataloging-in-Publication Data

Satie, Erik, 1866–1925
    [Correspondence. English]
    Satie seen through his letters/[edited by] Ornella Volta;
    translated by Michael Bullock; introduction by John Cage.
    Bibliography: p.
    Includes index.
    1. Satie, Erik, 1866–1925 — Correspondence. 2. Composers — France
— Correspondence.   I. Volta, Ornella.   II. Title.
ML410.S196A4 1988
780'.92'4 — dc19   87-26872
[B]   MN

ISBN 0-7145-2811-0 Cloth

Typeset in Baskerville 11/13pt and Futura by Ann Buchan (Typesetters)
Printed and bound in Great Britain by The Camelot Press Ltd, Southampton

Contents

ACKNOWLEDGEMENT

I must express my thanks to the various owners of the letters reproduced in this book for their generous and invaluable contribution, most particularly:

Pierre-Marcel Adéma, Simone and André Albert-Sorel, Henri de Beaumont, Pierre-André Benoit, Marie and Pierre Bertin, Lisa Breton, Gabriella Buffet-Picabia, Robert Caby, Bronja and René Clair, Jean Denoël, Edouard Dermit, Arlette and Louis Durey, Edwin Engelberts, Nina Gubisch, Jacques Guérin, Léon Guichard, Arthur Hoérée, Lauretta and Jean Hugo, Etienne Labeyrie, Madeleine Li-Koechlin, Madeleine and Darius Milhaud, Claude Roland-Manuel, Olga Picabia, Henri Sauguet, Rosine Seringe, Dolly de Tinan, Christophe Tzara, André Veyssière, Suzanne and Jean Wiener, as well as Emmanuel Bondeville, Secrétaire perpétuel of the Académie des Beaux Arts, Institut de France, in 1983; François Chapon, Curator of the Bibliothèque Littéraire Jacques Doucet; François Lesure, Curator of the Département de la Musique de la Bibliothèque Nationale, in 1983; Bengt. Häger, Curator of the Dansmuseet; André Morel, President of the Fondation Erik Satie; Waine D. Shirley, Librarian of the Library of Congress; M. Lacandre, Curator of Documentation at the Musée National d'Art Moderne.

I am particularly grateful to the authors and the publishers of all the quoted texts and to Pierre-Daniel

Templier, Jean Roy, Anne de Margerie and Thierry Bodin, who unhesitatingly passed on to me the transcriptions, made in the past by themselves, of letters now scattered and, in some cases, possibly lost, as well as to Gavin Bryars, Antony Melville and Andrew Thomson for unpublished information they were kind enough to give me.

This book is dedicated to John Cage, who inspired it and was its first reader: the most attentive, stimulating and enlightened reader one could wish for.

Ornella Volta

BY WAY OF AN INTRODUCTION

John Cage to Ornella Volta

May 25, 1983

I have finished reading your book (in French: no English has arrived); I love it. I can say that of few others. Like yours they are profoundly touching: Norman Malcolm's *Memoir of Ludwig Wittgenstein* and Templier's *Erik Satie* (not in the English translation which I find impossible to read). This making reading matter touching must be what death does to biography. I remember Bucky Fuller telling me how Anne his wife nearly died and how he received from a convict in a California penitentiary a beautiful letter about love, that it depends on impermanence, that consoled him. For *mourir* you use *disparaître*. The closest word in English is *pass away*, an expression that would surely have disgusted Satie as much as it does everyone I know. I can imagine using *disappear* but it would only be puzzling. Death is better when attempts aren't made to hide it (treated as Satie did that of Socrates, or as you have that of Satie).

You have changed Satie for me. I now know so much more about him than I did before I read your book. I have a new lease on my love of him. I even have to get to know this new one. He is not tall as the photograph on plate XVI in Templier led me to believe; and he is in all aspects of his life, work, and relations to other people totally unpredictable (or do I not yet know him? should I have said mercurial?); on the other hand, he seems to have known very well the path he was on. I must read your book again; if not very soon in English, then once more in French. Did he actually make that remark to God, 'Le temps de passer un jupon, et je suis à vous'? The implied friendship makes me think of Thoreau on his deathbed. A visiting relative asked, 'Have you made your peace with God?' T[horeau] replied, 'I wasn't aware we had ever quarrelled'. There is, by the way, a beautiful book about T[horeau] by Walter Harding that is a collection of stories about him, pro and con, by people who actually knew him. It is *Thoreau, Man of Concord*. You are Satie's Walter Harding. He is Thoreau's Ornella Volta.

With love,

John

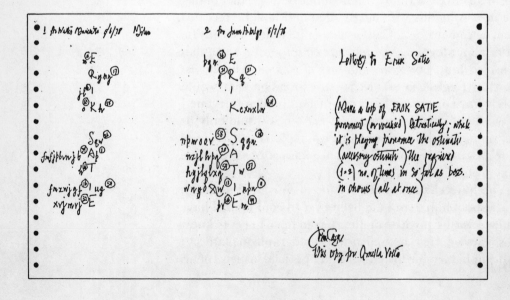

PREFACE

Apart from his music, letter-writing was Satie's favourite means of communication. It was by means of open letters in the press that he presented himself to Parisian Society; it was a lost letter that caused his last grief. It is through a bundle of letters that were never sent that we know the full extent of his one and only love. It was certain insults to a critic, sent through the post, that caused him the greatest difficulties he encountered. The urge to convey a message is at the centre of the only play he ever wrote, and it was in the form of letters that he set down his *causeries*, always with a formal heading at the beginning and expressions of politeness at the end. The day on which he wanted to draw his own attention to an important event, Satie did so by means of a letter addressed to himself, not forgetting to seal it, put a stamp on it and post it, in order to open and, no doubt, read it after the postman brought it back to him.

The style of this correspondence is modelled on the composer's concerns at the time he wrote it. Thus he made use of archaic expressions when advocating a return to the Gregorian chant in opposition to the Wagnerian 'Music of the Future', and of concise remarks at the time of his 'humorous' short piano pieces. Moreover, the graphic design of his missives (headed notepaper of impressive dimensions, the alternation of red and black ink, an unusual layout, or else letter cards of the most commonplace kind covered with a stiffly formal calligraphy) was perfectly suited to the masks of 'Parcier de l'Eglise Métropolitaine d'Art' or 'Bon Maître d'Arcueil', which Satie assumed at different periods, in each situation even using his clothes as a kind of aesthetic manifesto.

Whether they were addressed to an academician or to his brother, Satie's letters were always signed with his surname and forename, sometimes followed by his address even if the addressee was the occupant of the room next to his own. From the moment he reduced the size of the paper and the number of words, his signature was often replaced by a kind of logo: his initials harmoniously intertwined in the manner of the seals employed by the *fin-de-siècle* painters influenced by Japanese art.

Many of Satie's letters have been destroyed, concealed or lost. Those that still exist — even if, in some cases, only in the form of fragments — are nevertheless sufficient to give us a picture of the network of relationships which this recluse, who was actually very sociable, formed in the course of his life. We may say, therefore, that he always needed selected interlocutors — in order to express himself, and that every one of his works was conceived to answer the needs of a very precise environment. Let there be no mistake, however: it was always Satie who, by virtue of the work he bore within him, chose the environment most propitious to its realization.

If he was able to associate himself with the most varied trends, while maintaining a rare consistency, this was because, on the one hand, Satie was wise enough not to fear his own contradictions and, on the other, he always deliberately placed himself away from the centre of things. Accustomed as we are to seeing our recent history through the frequently distorting spectacles of its self-styled protagonists, it will prove both refreshing and salutary to look at it, in the course of these pages, from the — disarming and disarmed — point of view of this 'eccentric' figure.

Erik SATIE
Compositeur de Musique

BIRTH

The first letter we found relating to Erik Satie makes no mention of him. Its subject is the love at first sight that united his future parents.

The author of this letter is the father-to-be, Jules-Alfred Satie, known in the family as Alfred. At this time he was working as a ship-broker, following the examples of his father, Jules-André Satie, known in the family as Jules, and his younger brother, Louis-André, known in the family as André.

Alfred Satie was born at Honfleur (Calvados) in 1842. He studied in Lisieux, then spent a year in England and a second year in Norway for the purpose of learning the languages of these two countries, which were indispensable to the practice of his profession. Speaking perfect German, Portuguese, Spanish, Italian, Dutch, Danish, Latin and Greek (but having tried in vain to learn Russian), Alfred was later to find employment in Paris as a translator, first at the Foreign Ministry, then with an insurance company. At the age of eighteen he published, in the *Echo honfleurais*, under the pseudonym Silvio, several poems as well as articles on music in which he took the side of Rossini against Wagner.

In Paris he used his spare time to give piano and singing lessons with the aid of his second wife, Eugénie Barnetche, and quickly exhausted the inheritance from his father by setting himself up as a music publisher. He published several compositions by his wife, by his son Erik and by a friend of Erik's, Charles Levadé, who was later to become famous as the author of the comic opera *La Rôtisserie de la Reine Pedauque*. Alfred Satie also published some comic songs composed by himself for the stars of the Eden Concert, the Scala and the Alcazar d'Eté.

He died at Saint Germain en Laye, the birthplace of Debussy, at the age of sixty and, at his own request, received a secular burial.

At the Collège in Lisieux Alfred Satie had formed a lasting friendship with one of his schoolfellows, Albert Sorel, who was to become a very renowned historian, a member of the Institut and the Secretary General of the Présidence du Sénat, which gave him the right to live in the Château of Versailles. He belonged, like Alfred, to a Catholic family of Honfleur and, also like Alfred, married a foreign woman of the Protestant faith.

Alfred Satie to Albert Sorel

Honfleur, 25 March 1865

My Dear Albert,

The news I am about to give you will cause you no jubilation. I am on the point of marrying . . . guess who! You will never guess — Miss Jeannie Leslie Anton!!! When I say, 'on the point', I am perhaps being very premature. This is where we've got to: we have solemnly promised to wed. My father has not said yes, but he has not said *no*. He paid a *visit* to Miss Anton, to the satisfaction of both parties, and was *delighted* with the young woman; my mother is to see her tomorrow. We have only met three times at Miss Walworth's; we write to each other every day, and what letters! *Everything was done by correspondence and in two weeks!* To forestall some objections on your part, I can tell you that my father is entirely convinced

1.   that Miss Anton is very distinguished, has a very cultivated mind, is a good musician, and draws well;

2.   that she hasn't a cent;

3. that she never made any advances to me but, on the contrary, vigorously resisted my marriage proposals;
4. that her conduct has been the noblest and most disinterested imaginable;
5. that she loves me passionately.

You will ask me how all this happened. In the simplest and strangest manner. One fine day I wrote to Miss Anton, without knowing her except for having seen her once (without speaking to her) at Madame Bouton's, and having met her several times in the street, and I asked her if she would marry me. She hastened to say *no*, and wrote me the most discouraging letter imaginable. I was not discouraged: you know my liking for difficulties and problems. I returned to the attack and in the end I touched her heart — that's the whole story. Among other difficulties the religious one is not the least. My mother wants Miss Anton to promise that she will bring up her children in the Catholic faith, but Miss Anton vigorously refuses. There's no need for me to tell you that I am doing everything I can to support her resistance [. . .]

Alfred Satie

Jane Leslie Anton, known as Jeannie in the family, had been baptised in the Church of Scotland in London on 21 September 1838. Four years older than her husband — which was unusual at that time — she was the elder daughter of the corn and seed factor George Anton and the Scotswoman Elsie Davidson. The Gaelic name of her mother's family was MacDhaibhidh, their crest a stag's head, their plant badge red whortleberry, their motto *Sapienter si sincere* ('Wise if sincere') and their traditional tune *Tulloch Castle*. Jane's second forename, which she passed on to her elder son, links her to the Clan Leslie, originally from Aberdeenshire and known throughout Europe for its acts and declarations in favour of Scottish independence. The Leslie crest is a demi-griffin, their plant badge rue, their motto *'Grip fast'*.

It was less than four months after writing to Albert Sorel that Alfred Satie put his plan into execution. On 20 July 1865 *The Times* carried an announcement that on the previous day he had been joined in wedlock to Jane Leslie Anton by the Rev John Jessopp M.R., chaplain to His Majesty the King of the Belgians, at St Mary's Church in Barnes in Surrey.

The very fact that the ceremony took place in England seems to indicate that at this time the difficulties encountered by Alfred in the bosom of the family had not yet been entirely resolved. Nevertheless, on the following 15 September the marriage was recorded at the registry office of Honfleur, where the young couple, after honeymooning in Scotland, had moved into the house with Alfred's parents in the rue Haute. In this street which — contrary to its name — is the lowest in the town, the first of their four children, 'Monsieur' Eric Alfred Leslie, was born on 17 May 1866. An anomaly for the period, this child was not baptised — at the Anglican Church of Honfleur — until more than three months later, on 29 August.

Known in the family as Eric, at his majority he changed the final 'c' of his name to 'k', following the Scandinavian spelling, no doubt to underline the fact that the Normans are 'little Vikings'.

Erik Satie came into the world, as he said later, 'very young in very old times'. Though he declared also that he was 'bald from birth', early photographs and pictures show that he started life with a reasonable quantity of reddish fair hair which, as the years went by, turned a deep chestnut colour before thinning considerably. By his own account, his eyes were 'grey (probably specked)' while others insist that they were blue. The maximum height he attained at the time of his military service was 1m.67 (5′ 7″).

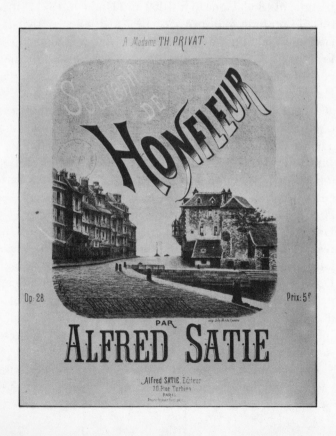

SCHOOLS

Madame Alfred Satie, neé Jane Leslie Anton, insisted upon an Anglican baptism for the four children to whom she gave birth: Eric Alfred Leslie in 1866, Louise Olga Jeannie in 1868, Conrad in 1869 and Diane in 1871. Since this did nothing to improve relations with her mother-in-law, her husband, on his return from the war against the Prussians (in which, he was anxious to point out, he had not killed anyone), decided to leave his native town. Having abandoned his activities as a ship-broker, he accepted the employment which Albert Sorel had offered him in Paris soon after the tragic event of the Commune. The following year, when Eric was only six, Diane and Jane Leslie both died, a few weeks apart. Before departing for Milan and Lübeck to forget his grief, Alfred Satie entrusted his daughter Olga to a maternal uncle in Le Havre and Eric and Conrad to his own parents in Honfleur. The grandparents only agreed to look after the two orphans on condition that they renounce the Anglican faith and receive Catholic baptism. This was done on 4 December 1872 in the presence of the Mayor of Honfleur, in St Catherine's Church, which had been built at the end of the Hundred Years War to celebrate the departure of the English. The officiant, the Rev Dallibert, had been furnished with a special permit by the Bishop of Lisieux.

Eric became a boarder at the Collège of Honfleur in the rue de l'Homme de Bois, two streets higher up than the rue Haute, where he seems to have scored no noteworthy successes beyond a certificate of merit, third class, in vocal music, bestowed in the course of a public ceremony on 6 August 1878. At the end of this same summer his grandmother was to meet an accidental death while bathing in the sea. Eric then returned to Paris to live with his father who, for three months, took him everywhere with him, notably to certain courses in literature and philosophy at the Collège de France and the Sorbonne as well as to receptions given by Albert Sorel at Versailles. Here Alfred Satie met Eugénie Barnetche, a music teacher with whom, in keeping with his impulsive nature, he quickly established, on 21 January 1879, a new home where rooms were also found for little Conrad and Eugénie's mother.

Eric had taken music lessons from the organist of St Leonard's church in Honfleur, one Monsieur Vinot, a graduate of the École Niedermeyer (who was dedicated to the restoration of the Gregorian chant) and a composer of

Leçons d'Allemand
et de Musique
M. VINOT, professeur
Rue Bourdet, n° 32.

Conservatoire National
de Musique
et de Déclamation.

M. Satie est admis Élève à la Classe de Piano de M. Mathias. Il y entrera le
Ce 6 novembre 1885.

Le Directeur,
Ambroise Thomas

Art. 40 du Règlement. — Les Élèves ne sont d'abord admis que provisoirement. Leur admission définitive n'est prononcée qu'après l'examen semestriel qui suit celui de leur admission provisoire.

IMAGERIE PELLERIN   COMPAGNIE D'INFANTERIE DE LIGNE   IMAGERIE D'EPINAL. N° 109bis
EN MARCHE & AU FEU - TENUE DE CAMPAGNE

slow waltzes. Noting the child's natural bent for music, which led to his being nicknamed 'Crin-Crin' (scraper), his stepmother enrolled him, on 4 November 1879, at the Conservatoire National de Musique et de Déclamation in Paris, 'a huge, very uncomfortable and rather ugly building, a sort of local penitentiary without any exterior charm — or interior either', according to him.

Eight years later, not having obtained any diploma from this institution, young Satie found a way of escaping from it by volunteering for service in the Army. After joining the 33rd Infantry Regiment at Arras, he soon took the step of going outdoors one winter night without even a shirt on in order to contract bronchitis, which, though brought about his discharge from the Army, became chronic.

The following letter, which may or may not have reached the addressee, expresses the way he felt about the instruction he received.

Erik Satie to the Conservatoire National
de Musique et de Déclamation

Paris, 17 November of 92

Individual Theme of Liturgical Chastity
by the High Wisdom with which I am filled,
I speak to you

Hear ye:

A child, I entered your classes; My spirit was so gentle that
you could not understand it: and My way of walking around
astonished the flowers, for they thought they were seeing an
artificial zebra.*

And despite My extreme youth and My delicious agility,
through your unintelligence you made Me detest the coarse
art which you teach, by your inexplicable harshness you
made me for a long time despise you.

Now that all the External Vegetation** is in Me, I absolve
you of your faults in regard to Me; I pray the Lord to forgive
you; I bless the unhappy souls which you will educate until
the day when the Capital Power will take them from your
profane hands and restore them to the Seraphim of the
Virgin Mary.

I have spoken.

Erik Satie

* taken as the apparition of a sympathetic being
** this indicates My great sensitivity to the things of Nature

When nearly forty, Satie went back to school, at a time
when the idea of continuing education was not yet
current. A vague feeling of dissatisfaction, coupled with
two events that significantly affected him — the
performance of Debussy's *Pelléas et Mélisande*, the final
emergence of an aesthetic to whose formulation he had
contributed, and the death of his father — had impelled
him to start all over again from the very beginning.

In October 1905, therefore, he decided to enroll at the
Schola Cantorum, which was devoted primarily to

religious music. Banned from the Conservatoire, Bach and Palestrina here occupied places of honour. As a former student of this institution, Louis Laloy, has explained: 'Harmony was not taught at the Schola. Counterpoint had to suffice us, as it had sufficed the musicians of the Middle Ages. It was, I believe, Monsieur Vincent d'Indy, who must be held responsible for this prejudice in favour of the archaic.'

Having made his choice, Satie found himself confronted by an obstacle of a financial nature. Faced with the need to make good a serious deficit, the Schola demanded high fees from its students.

Erik Satie to Vincent d'Indy
Director of the Schola Cantorum

[September 1905]

Monsieur le Président,

I the undersigned have the honour to address to the benevolent Administrative Council of your gracious institution an application for a scholarship that will enable me to take M. Albert Roussel's course in counterpoint.

I am a poor artist contending with the difficulties of life and I deeply regret not being able to pay the fees required by your fine school because it is absolutely impossible for me to find the sum required of students taking these courses.

Please accept, Monsieur le Président, my respectful salutations

Erik Satie

Albert Roussel, who was four years younger than Satie, was astonished by his decision. What could he teach him that he did not know already? His new pupil was to prove, for three years, 'very willing and diligent'.

'He was conscientious in handing over the homework he had written out with such care, adding annotations in red ink. He was profoundly musical,' observed Roussel.

Erik Satie to Albert Roussel

Arcueil, 6 October 1907

Dear Monsieur Roussel,

How are you?

What a long time it is since I had the pleasure of seeing you. It seems far away, lost in time. We have a new periodical, *Comoedia*, which is quite funny. Willy, the good Willy, is involved in it. *Tant mieux.*

Will you forgive me for not attending your first class of the new term?

I shan't be able to come until Wednesday 9 October. You will forgive me, won't you? It's not my fault.

I shall bring a canon, or something claiming to be such.

Your affectionate pupil

Erik Satie

On 15 June 1908, at the age of forty-two, Satie received the first diploma of his life. Above the signatures of Vincent d'Indy, director of the Schola, Albert Roussel, the class teacher, and Jean de La Laurencie, the general secretary, it states that 'Monsieur Erik Satie, a pupil in the course in counterpoint, has passed the end-of-year examinations with distinction and fulfils the conditions required for devoting himself exclusively to the study of composition.' Twenty years had already gone by since the composition of the *Gymnopédies*.

In order to put his new knowledge to use, Satie then composed a fugue. His friend Debussy, who had already commented ironically on his new commitment by dedicating a copy of *Images* 'to the famous contrapuntist', immediately wrote to a Portuguese musician, a former instructor at the Schola, who had just been appointed orchestra leader at Montreux.

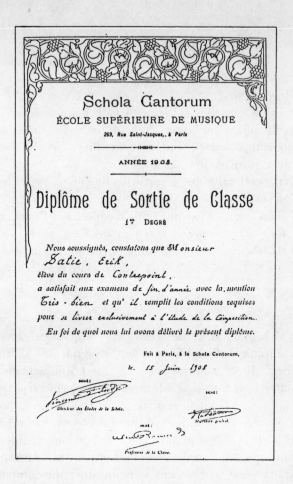

Claude Debussy to Francisco de Lacerda

5 September 1908

Dear Friend,

I was very happy to hear of your appointment [. . .]. Does it not seem to you preferable to breathe the air of Montreux instead of the vestry-scented air of the 'Schola'?

In this connection, your friend E. Satie has just completed a fugue in which tedium is concealed behind malevolent harmonies, in which you will recognize the mark of the special discipline that characterizes the aforesaid establishment [. . .].

Claude Debussy

No doubt the person most concerned was informed of this unflattering evaluation of his work, for, after adding to the 'fugue' in question a *Choral* and a *Pastorale* that owed nothing to Beethoven, he entitled these three pieces *Aperçus désagréables* [Unpleasant glimpses]. He had, by the way, noted reactions similar to Debussy's on the part of Ravel and his disciples, the Jeunes Ravêlites.

A founder of the Société Musicale Indépendante, Ravel was actually on the look-out for talents neglected by the Société Nationale de Musique (from which he had resigned with a flourish) in order to demonstrate its conservatism. The 'discovery' of Erik Satie formed part of this strategy. That was why, rather than support those works of Satie's that were the fruit of his studies at the Schola, directed by d'Indy — who was also one of the mandarins of the Société Nationale — Ravel preferred to promote the works of Satie's youth, which had the added advantage of proving that Debussy (Ravel's true rival in the Parisian musical world) had not invented the whole thing.

Having resumed relations with his brother after a quarrel lasting for several years, Satie acquainted him with these various ups and downs, without having yet fully grasped his unexpected promoters' true motives.

Erik Satie to Conrad Satie

Arcueil, 17 January 1911

[. . .] What have I been doing all this long time? Miracles, *mon pauvre vieux*! So many things have happened to me that I don't know where I stand. Among the unpleasant events I will list the floods that have coldly disturbed my existence and especially personal and private finances, not merely reducing me to a poverty which I dislike, but also making it impossible for me to fulfil my engagements.

You know that I have composed *café-concert* music.

I gave this sort of music up long ago.

That was no field for me to be working in. It is more stupid and dirty than anything.

In 1905 I put myself to work with d'Indy. I was tired of being reproached with an ignorance of which I thought I must be guilty, since competent people pointed it out in my works.

After three years of hard work I obtained from the Schola Cantorum my diploma in counterpoint, signed by my excellent master, who is certainly the most knowledgeable and the best man in this world.

Here I am then, in 1908, holding a certificate that gives me the title of contrapuntist. Proud of my knowledge, I set to work to compose. My first work of this kind is a *Choral & fugue* for four hands. I have often been insulted in my poor life, but never was I so despised. What on earth had I been doing with d'Indy? The things I wrote before had such charm! Such depth! And now? How boring and uninteresting!

Whereupon the 'Jeunes' mounted a campaign against d'Indy and played the *Sarabandes* and *Le Fils des Etoiles*, and so on, works that were once considered the fruits of a profound ignorance — wrongly, according to these 'Jeunes'.

That's life, *mon vieux*!

It's total nonsense.

While I was studying I gave lessons and earned a royal living.

Then, *crac*! Poverty arrived like a sad little girl with large green eyes . . .

Erik Satie

BEGINNINGS

Although he entered it for the sole purpose of escaping the constraints of the Conservatoire, military service at Arras was not entirely useless to Satie. There he made the acquaintance of the local painter Armand Robert who was a friend of a Paris plumber, Vital Hocquet. The latter devoted his leisure hours to writing poetry under the name of Narcisse Lebeau.

In December 1887 it was the plumber-poet who launched Satie into the artistic and literary cabaret Le Chat Noir, situated in Paris at the foot of Montmartre. Satie introduced himself to Rodolphe Salis, the redoubtable director of this establishment, as a *gymnopédiste*. 'That's a fine profession,' replied Salis without batting an eyelid. Having passed the rite of passage into this establishment, which was not open to just anyone, the composer had no alternative but to write the three *Gymnopédies* which were to justify, retroactively, the title that he had claimed. The comment at the Chat Noir was that this work seemed to have been composed 'by a savage with good taste'. Etymologically, the *gymnopédie* was a dance performed in Sparta, in honour of Apollo, by 'naked children'. Attached as it is to one of Erik Satie's best known works, this title has today come to be looked upon as proper to the 'nakedness' of his music.

Satie had come across the word in a poem by one of his friends, J.P. Contamine de Latour, *Les Antiques*, from

which he took the following lines as an epigraph to the first *Gymnopédie* when he published it, the following summer, in *La Musique des Familles*: Oblique et coupant l'ombre un torrent éclatant/Ruisselait en flots d'or sur la dalle polie/Où les atomes d'ambre su feu se miroitant/Mêlaient leur sarabande à la gymnopédie. [Aslant and slashing the shadow a dazzling torrent/Flowed in golden waves across the polished floor/Where atoms of amber sparkling in the firelight/Mingled their saraband with the gymnopédie].'

Drawn some time later, a sketch in red chalk shows Satie with a conductor's baton in his hand. This arose from the fact that Victor-Dynam Fumet — who, until then had conducted concert versions of operas and other music, used to accompany the shadow shows presented at the Chat Noir — had quarrelled with Salis and passed on his baton to Satie. Fumet, whose works of this period present some similarities to Satie's, was nicknamed 'Dynam' because of his sympathy with the anarchists, who at that time were known for their immoderate use of dynamite. Victor-Dynam later went in for alchemical experiments and even obtained a grant from a princess so

that he could devote himself undisturbed to the
manufacture of 'gold'. At the end of his life he was the
organist of a Paris church and a religious bigot.

In the sketch showing Satie as a conductor — as in all
his portraits of the period — Satie is wearing a frock-coat
and a top-hat. A long ribbon of black silk is attached to his
pince-nez. This entirely respectable get-up, which was,
however, contradicted by the tattered old trousers that,
with pair of military boots that could only have been left
over from his brief stay in the army, earned him the
nickname 'Monsieur le Pauvre' (Mr Poverty). This
nickname was to prove increasingly appropriate, since the
composer made poverty a matter of aesthetic principle.
Thirty years later the 'pauvre' music of Erik Satie was to
serve as a banner for young French music.

At the same time he was launched into society
(represented by the Chat Noir), Satie left his family. His
father who, in his capacity of amateur music publisher,
had just published his first songs, gave him sixteen
hundred francs to help him set up his own home. 'It was a
respectable sum,' commented his friend Contamine de
Latour, 'for a young man accustomed to scrape by on a
hundred sous a week. It seemed that it would never end.
Satie rented a small mezzanine flat and filled it with
choice furniture. Then he had to lower his sights. The
furniture disappeared piece by piece as his capital
dwindled.' Soon he had to move from this first residence
(50 rue Condorcet, near the Chat Noir) to the very top of
the Butte Monmartre which at this time was completely
rural. He felt very comfortable up there, he said, because
it placed him 'well above his creditors'.

The Chat Noir was the first public, or even private,
place in Paris where esoteric poets and humorists, church
painters and *chansonniers*, princes of the blood and simple
workmen mingled without discrimination. There Satie
met, among others, the spirited writer Alphonse Allais (a
native of Honfleur like himself), the illustrator Maurice
Radiguet (a contributor, as Marcel Duchamp was to be

later, to the revue *Le Rire*, and the future father of the poet and novelist Raymond Radiguet) as well as 'one of the seven uncles' of Blaise Cendrars. The medieval decor of this cabaret was particularly well suited to Erik Satie, described by another friend he met around this time, Claude Debussy, as 'a gentle medieval musician who turned up in our century'. The Chat Noir published a

periodical of the same name, edited by its habitués who made use of it to impose a characteristic form of wit.

The success of the Chat Noir inspired many imitators. In a few years there were countless 'cabarets artistiques et littéraires' at the foot of the Butte, each one trying to give itself a different style. At the Aristide Bruant's Mirliton, the melodramatic stories narrated by Zola or painted by Steinlen were turned into songs; the Divan Japonais' sign was in line with the fashion for the exotic which then dominated contemporary French painting. After the manner of the Japanese, beloved by painters he befriended, Satie searched for beauty through a minimum of means.

At the Divan Japonais, according to a guidebook of the period, 'everything is Chinese: in this hoax in the best taste, an attempt has been made to render it more piquant by entrusting the service to Japanese ladies — even more Chinese than all the rest — you will find the equipment of a Paris café converted by a change of decor into objects from a bazaar in Japan. The billiard table is painted blue and red and has bamboo rods stuck to it. The gas burners are decorated with little bells, large panels of silk have been hung on the walls.' This picturesque establishment was run by a man from Lyon, Jean Sarrazin, who called himself *Jehan* and was nicknamed 'the olive poet' because he had gained popularity by peddling olives in the cafés, wrapped in paper on which he had first scribbled poems of his own composition. Jehan Sarrazin, like the other directors of Parisian cabarets, had also endowed the Divan Japonais with a periodical, *La Lanterne Japonaise*.

We must suppose that Satie had access to the *Lanterne Japonaise* as well as to the *Chat Noir*, since between the end of 1888 and the beginning of 1889 these two periodicals did their utmost to increase the fame of this beginner who had just published his first works at his own expense.

Le Chat Noir
VII, No 7, 24 November 1888
Erik Satie's *Gymnopédie No 3* has just been published from 66 boulevard Magenta. We cannot too strongly recommend to the musical public this essentially artistic work which is justly considered one of the finest of the century in which this unfortunate gentleman is born.

La Lanterne Japonaise
I, No 6, 1 December 1888
We receive from all sides letters asking us where the Complete Works of Erik Satie may be found.
Once and for all, the definitive edition of the subtle melodies of this composer are not yet in production.
Nevertheless, in return for a ridiculously small sum the first-comer will find the *Gymnopédie No 3* (one of the most beautiful) at 66 boulevard Magenta.
Let this resound in all heads.

Le Chat Noir
VIII, No 369, 9 February 1889
At last! Lovers of cheerful music can give themselves endless pleasure. The indefatigable Erik Satie, the sphinx man, the woodenheaded composer, announces the appearance of a new musical work which, up till now, he says, is the greatest. It is a series of melodies conceived, in the mystico-liturgical mode beloved of the author, under the suggestive title *Ogives*. We wish Erik Satie a success comparable to the one he has already attained with his *Gymnopédie No 3*, currently under all pianos.
On sale at 66 boulevard Magenta.

La Lanterne Japonaise
II, No 15, 23 March 1889
Japanese Salad
M. Erik Satie, musical composer, received the following letter, which he has asked us to print:

Précigny-les-Balayettes, 20 February 1889

Sir,

For eight years I have suffered from a polyp in the nose, complicated by a liver disorder and rheumatic pains.

On hearing your *Ogives* my condition showed a clear improvement. Four or five applications of your *Gymnopédie No 3* cured me completely.

I hereby authorize you, Monsieur Erik Satie, to make any use of this testimonial you may wish.

In the meantime please accept the thanks of your grateful

Femme Lengrenage
Day worker at Précigny-les-Balayettes

As for us, our opinion of M. Erik Satie, whom we do not have the honour of knowing personally, can be summed up in four words: he's a hot rabbit!

FRIENDS

Erik Satie copied the letter he addressed to the Conservatoire into a small music exercise book, in which he also wrote out the first version of the ballet *Uspud*, composed in collaboration with the poet J.P. Contamine de Latour, and the letters he exchanged with Latour in the process.

J.P. Contamine de Latour to Erik Satie
progenitor of Sublimities

Lutèce, the 17th day of
the grey November of 1800 + 92

Mon bien affectionné Ami,

   despite the Evils of winter I send thee the libretto of *Uspud*, this *mystique* and *mi-chrétien* ballet that is the object of thine lofty desires; and this because thou art my brother in humanity, and because nothing that touches upon the regeneration of intelligence is alien to me, insofar as I have been initiated by thee.

   Uspud is not a psychological or even an immaterial fact, but the pale reflection of souls set free from the terrible Heaviness and whom thirst for love conquered by the purification of the senses in pain renders indifferent to the world; as such, it minimizes the most intense expression of moral heroism and is above the appreciation of anyone here below.

I do not seek either approbation or criticism, but the inner peace consented to by the common man who feeds on it; and for this reason I wish to have around me peace, withdrawal, silence and for thee the sanctification of the blessed or Eternity.

And out of Respect, Deference and Veneration, I thou thee

J.P. Contamine de Latour

Erik Satie to J.P. Contamine de Latour
Supernatural in Writings
the 17th of the month of November of 92
Friendly theme of Superiority and Certitude
Immense Benefactor
By the True Sign of the Cross of Jesus,
Greetings:

After having told Me to walk during the fifty-two Red Months, you left, looking at Me with eyes turned inward.* And as you foretold, My right hand has become sonorous, and My head has acquired a sensibility it did not possess before; also joy is on My clothes and in My food.

I owe it to you, Immense Benefactor, that I have seen the Puffed Up One** stretch out his arms on which there were no longer any hairs; and then My penetration broke, which is an unforgettable Pride. I restore Myself and abase Myself before your Sacrilegious Song.

And out of respect, deference and veneration I say to you: 'Vous'.

Erik Satie

* as a sign of deep meditation
** means the totality of the Pretentious

J.P. Contamine de Latour (as he signed most of his short stories, plays, poems and newspaper articles without ever revealing what the initials stood for) was in reality called José Maria Vicente Ferrer Francisco de Paula Patricio Manuel Contamine, and known as 'Patrice' to his

intimates. He was born in Tarragona, Spain, on 17 March 1867, ten months precisely after Erik Satie, and was to die in Paris ten months after Satie on 23 May 1926. He claimed to be related to Napoleon and hence to be entitled to the throne of France. His brother had to obtain for his own children the legal right to the name 'Contamine de Latour', which Patrice had only been able to use as a pen name. He married three times, the third time on his deathbed. His elder sister, Maria de la Concepción, Patrocinia, Barbara Contamine, married Henry Pacory who was also the author of words for songs by Satie.

Erik Satie and Patrice Contamine came to know each other 'thanks to one of those insignificant persons whom chance uses in order to bring together kindred beings'. It was together that they discovered the Chat Noir, and spent many nights and days creating joint works, imagining esoteric sects and planning practical jokes. There were even times when they could only go out into the street one at a time, because they had only one respectable suit between them. Satie called Patrice 'le Vieux Modeste', or else 'Ch'timi', which means 'Cher ami' in the dialect of the town of Arras, where he did his military service.

In 1888 Contamine de Latour dedicated to Satie a booklet, *Parfum d'Avril*, and in 1889 *Miriam*, the first of his *Cinq Nouvelles*. He wrote out verses of his own on the manuscript of Satie's first *Sarabande* and inspired the title of the *Gymnopédies*.

A few poems by J.P. Contamine de Latour were set to music by Satie and others by Charles Levadé. Satie composed *Uspud*, a 'Christian ballet', to a libretto signed by his friend, as well as theatre music for *Monsieur Mouche* and *Geneviève de Brabant*, two plays written by Patrice Contamine under the pseudonym Lord Cheminot.

On Satie's death, J.P. Contamine published the moving *Souvenirs de Jeunesse* in *Comoedia* in which he recounted the epic story of *Uspud*.

The apogee of the symbiosis between composer and librettist, this ballet was written for the Auberge du Clou shadow theatre, directed by Miguel Utrillo. The latter was the presumptive father of Maurice Utrillo, son of Suzanne Valadon, and formed a group of Spanish painters in Montmartre with Ignacio Zuloaga, Santiago Rusiñol and Ramón Casas, all friends of Satie.

Cut to the quick by the mockery of the Auberge du Clou customers over the thinness of the score for *Uspud*, Satie had bet them that he would get his work performed at the Paris Opera.

Having received no reply to a first request for an interview addressed to the director of this institution, he wrote again several times adopting a more and more threatening tone, not omitting to deal out copies of his letters at the Clou.

Erik Satie to Monsieur Bertrand
director of the Théâtre National de l'Opéra

[November 1892]

I cannot believe, Sir, that your silence is the result of negligence or prejudice, otherwise your attitude would call for punishment.

As a civil servant entrusted with looking after the interests of Music, it is not permissible for you to dismiss a work without knowing it.

If such were the case, I should feel compelled to appeal to Monsieur le Ministre de l'Instruction Publique et des Beaux Arts, and your persistence in refusing me an answer would assume the character of a personal insult for which I should be obliged to demand satisfaction with weapons [. . .]

When this letter still failed to produce the desired result, Satie decided to take extreme measures.

Erik Satie to Monsieur Bertrand
director of the Théâtre National de l'Opéra

[December 1892]

The benevolence which, in spite of everything, I feel towards you impels me to accord you a further and final delay of one week. Once this period is passed I shall regretfully have to address to the Minister the expression of my just indignation and to send two of my friends to call upon you to account for your conduct.

Erik Satie

A few days later, two sombre-looking confederates (Patrice Contamine and André Mycho, son of the painter-engraver Marcellin Desboutin and, like his father, one of Satie's portraitists) called at Monsieur Bertrand's private home to leave their visiting cards, accompanied by threatening remarks. The following day Satie received a note from the director of the Paris Opera, apologizing for this tardiness in replying and inviting the two authors to bring him their work.

Erik Satie to Ernest Legrand

Paris, the 18th of the month of December 1892

Mon cher & venerable Maître,

[...] Bertrand received me yesterday together with Latour; this leads me to believe in the early performance of *Uspud* at the Opera in the winter of 1927 or, at the latest, that of 1943.

A toi de tout coeur et d'esprit

Erik Satie

Satie's predictions were still to prove over-optimistic. *Uspud* was not, in fact, staged until 1979. Nevertheless the composer won his bet, since this performance did take place at the Opéra Comique, on the initiative of one of Bertrand's successors, Rolf Liebermann.

On that day of December 1892 Satie could in any case consider himself satisfied. To have compelled the director of the Opera to handle him with kid gloves was an important point gained. In order to make those around him better appreciate this victory, and also to preserve its memory, he conceived the idea of having the libretto printed and illustrated with extracts from the score, stating on the title page that this work had been, if not *représenté* at least *présenté* at the Opera.

As for the publication costs, the habitués of the Clou and other acquaintances were invited to raise a subscription. Having failed to respond with sufficient alacrity, Reynaldo Hahn received the following enraged epistle, decorated with flaming hearts, swords and other symbols drawn in red Chinese ink:

Reynaldo chante "l'Île Heureuse"

Erik Satie to Reynaldo Hahn
In the name of the Rose + Cross
curses upon you!
Erik Satie

The manuscript of *Uspud* was offered to the friend who had more closely followed events.

Erik Satie to Ernest Le Grand de la Motte Houdon
Marquis de Sailleuse Lubert
Member of the National Society of Agriculture
Composer of Music

To my good old Ernest Le Grand I offer this precious manuscript made specially for the unique glorification of the Lord My Infinite Father;

may he accept it from My splendid hands, may he respect it always; that is what I wish.
His brother in creation
Erik Satie

Ernest Legrand had known Satie at the Conservatoire. A composer of rare quality, he is said to have destroyed the greater part of his own work. Legrand had to make a gift of the manuscript of *Uspud* to another musician he admired.

Ernest Legrand to an unidentified friend
Paris, 22 May [19]34

[. . .] Allow me to present you with a small rectangular record which, if you turn it, will nevertheless remain silent.

It is the only souvenir I have left of a being whom I revered for his talent and the charm of his conversation, which was almost divine [. . .].
Ernest Legrand

LOVE

The edition of *Uspud* published by Satie is characterized, on the one hand, by the exclusive use of lower case letters (for the first time, to our knowledge, in the history of typography) and, on the other, by the design on its cover: the reproduction of a charcoal drawing signed by Suzanne Valadon showing the profiles of the two authors, Erik Satie and Contamine de Latour, enclosed in a circle as though designed for a medallion.

Two years later, Satie published the same extracts from the score of *Uspud* for the second time in an even smaller format. The medallion designed by Valadon was once more used for the cover, with the difference that this time the artist's signature was omitted.

In the meantime, in fact, something had happened.

Born in 1865, a year before Satie, Marie Clémentine Valadon, known as Suzanne Valadon, had chosen to be a painter after having been first a trapeze artist and then a model for Renoir, Puvis de Chavannes and Toulouse-Lautrec. In 1883 she had a son, Maurice, whose father — as he admitted seven years later — was the painter and art critic Miguel Utrillo y Morlius. Utrillo and Valadon posed for several pictures by Santiago Rusiñol. One of them, painted in 1891, shows Utrillo dressed in an infantry-man's uniform borrowed from Satie. It was, no doubt, through Utrillo that Satie met Valadon. A brief but intense relationship developed, the essential stages of which are set out in the following notice ornately handwritten by Satie:

> On the 14th of the month of January in the year of grace 1893, which was a Saturday, my love affair with Suzanne Valadon began, which ended on Tuesday the 20th of June of the same year.
>
> On Monday 16 of the month of January 1893, my friend Suzanne Valadon came to this place for the first time in her life and on Saturday 17 June of the same year for the last.

According to two different versions of what happened which he gave to friends years later, it was Satie who took the initiative in breaking off the relationship — although we know that immediately afterwards Valadon moved in with the banker Paul Mousis, whom she later married. According to the first version, one fine day Satie went to the local police station and asked for protection from this lady who was harassing him. According to the second, he had personally pushed Valadon out of the window into the courtyard of the building and had then gone to the police to accuse himself of 'murder' — wrongly, he pointed out, because her past experience as an acrobat had enabled her to come out unscathed, both from his window and from his life.

As direct witness to Satie's feelings only two letters remain, the first addressed to Suzanne at a particularly delicate moment in their relationship, the second sent to Conrad Satie when it was all over.

The letter to Valadon was written with a carefully designed layout on paper distinguished by a coat of arms in peacock blue, showing a chicken with the motto: 'Aigle ne puis, dindon ne daigne, poule suis.' (Eagle I cannot, turkey I do not deign, chicken I am.) Before making a present of this letter to one of her friends (Dr Robert Le Masle, the French translator of Rollo Myers' biography of Satie), Valadon carefully removed her name and address.

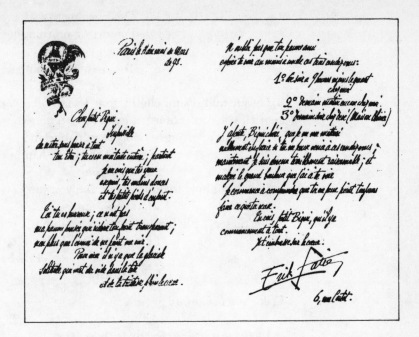

It must be noted that this address, 6 rue Cortot, was the same as Satie's, as the latter had not failed to indicate once more under his signature.

Erik Satie to Suzanne Valadon

Paris, the 11th of the month of March 93

Dear little Biqui,

Impossible
to stop thinking about your whole
being; you are in Me complete; everywhere,
I see nothing but your exquisite
eyes, your gentle hands
and your little child's feet.

You, you are happy; My poor thoughts
are not going to wrinkle your transparent forehead;
any more than worry at not seeing Me.

For Me there is only the icy
solitude that creates an emptiness in my head
and fills my heart with sorrow.

Don't forget that your poor friend
hopes to see you at least at one of these three rendezvous:

    1.   This evening at 8.45 at my place
    2.   Tomorrow morning again at my place
    3.   Tomorrow evening at Dédé's (Maison Olivier)

Let me add, Biqui chérie, that I shall on no account get angry if you can't come to any of these rendezvous;

I have now become terribly reasonable; and

    in spite of the great happiness it gives me to see you

I am beginning to understand that you can't always do what you want.

    You see, little Biqui, there is a beginning to everything.
    I kiss you on the heart

            Erik Satie

  6, rue Cortot

Erik Satie to Conrad Satie

               28 June 1893

I have just broken finally with Suzanne.
I shall have great difficulty in regaining possession of
    myself, loving this little
person as I have loved her ever since
    you left: she was able to take
      all of me.
Time will do what at this moment I cannot do [. . .]
            Erik Satie

After his brothers's death, Conrad Satie found a bundle of letters written by Satie to Suzanne Valadon but never sent to her. When advised of this discovery Valadon respnded with these few lines that, no doubt out of emotional excitement, she signed twice:

Suzanne Valadon to Conrad Satie

              [summer 1926]

Cher Ami,
   Your very friendly letter arrived just as I about to leave Paris — an emergency forces me to put off your visit — if

however you can — wait until the last week of August, for I should be back in Paris then.

The meeting will be a very moving one and so many memories are heart-rending indeed and yet very sweet to me.

Croyez, cher ami, en ma grande amitié

Suzanne Valadon
Suzanne Valadon

A date was finally fixed for delivery of the letters. After reading (and re-reading?) them, she burned them.

The love affair with Suzanne Valadon is the only one Satie is known ever to have had. 'Love is a sickness of the nerves,' he said one day to the painter Augustin Grass-Mick. 'It's serious, yes, very serious. . . Myself, I'm afraid of it, I avoid it. . .' Nevertheless in 1919, when Curnonsky asked him: 'What do you think about love?' he replied simply: 'I find it very comical.'

SECTS

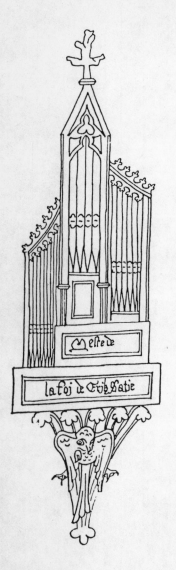

During one of the most difficult phases of his tumultuous relationship with Suzanne Valadon, Satie, 'for the great calm and profound tranquillity' of his soul, had composed a novena, *Danses gothiques*. The better to console himself for the end of this affaire he went so far as to found a new sect, of which he was himself to be the High Priest. He chose the esoteric periodical *Le Coeur* to publish this

First Epistle of Erik Satie
to Catholic Artists and to all Christians

My Brothers:

We live in unsettled times when Western society, daughter of the Apostolic and Roman Catholic Church, is invaded by the shades of impiety, a thousand times more barbarous than in the days of Paganism, and seems close to perishing. We can only watch with regret as men offend God every day by their ignorance of the divine precepts of the Gospel and distance themselves from fervour, continence, Holy practices and pious customs; We are saddened to see them listening to those who come to manifest their diabolic works and their lies; We censure them for being guilty of pride, impenitence and malignity to the supreme degree, instead of mortifying, by dint of suffering, all that remains in them of the earthly; and We are dissatisfied no longer to see them fighting for the glory of God, the honour of the Church and the edification of the public. Daring to attribute to these causes the evils with which We are afflicted, Our Christian heart has been moved to see the misfortune of so many souls that are going to eternal damnation; it has drawn from the infinite grace of Our Lord Jesus Christ the ardent desire to work for their sanctification by the means best calculated to restore Holy Religion, which the evil are trampling underfoot, and the Arts which are its most sublime expression.

We are therefore resolved, in accord with Our conscience and confident in the mercy of God, to erect in the metropolis of this Frankish nation, which for so many centuries has claimed the glorious title of Elder Daughter of the Church, a Temple worthy of the Saviour, conductor and redeemer of the peoples; We shall make of it a refuge where Catholicism and the Arts that are indissolubly linked to it shall grow and prosper, sheltered from all profanation and in the complete flowering of their purity, which the efforts of the Evil One will be unable to tarnish.

After mature reflection, We have given this refuge of revivified Faith the name *Eglise Métropolitaine d'Art* and have placed it under the divine invocation of *Jésus Conducteur*. The first and inestimable expression of affectionate gratitude and Christian approbation that a great number of Our brothers have deigned to convey to Us have spread in Our heart both an ineffable joy and a fortifying seed of courage to resist the snares which Hell might set for Us.

We therefore beg you, My Brothers, in the name of the Salvation of Humanity as of Our own Salvation, to join with Us for the triumph of Our Holy Mother the Church by the purification of Faith and the Arts, which are one of the ways by which Providence calls us to Her; and We kiss you in the Peace and Fraternity of Jesus Christ Our Lord.

Erik Satie

given in Paris in October 1893, the 15th

In relation to his church, Satie named himself *Parcier* (an ancient form of *partiaire* or 'shareholder') and *Maître de Chapelle*. The fact that he remained the sole member did not deter him from setting down on paper the titles and the respective costumes of an ecclesiastical hierarchy exceeding one thousand six hundred million individuals in number. The only evidence we have of the doctrine he preached comes to us from Santiago Rusiñol who, one day in January 1894, saw him in ecstasy between two canvases by El Greco (*Las Lágrimas de San Pedro* and *Santa María Magdalena en Omracció*, now at the Museo du Cau Ferrat at Sitges), because, according to him, they 'perfectly expressed the aim he had set himself in founding his Church, which consisted in combating society by means of music and painting'.

The title of Parcier de l'Eglise Métropolitaine d'Art had finally provided Satie with the pedestal that official institutions had refused him. He lost no time in making use of it to hurl anathemata at the most prominent intellectuals. One of his favourite targets was Aurélien Lugné-Poe, founder and manager of the Théâtre de l'Oeuvre de la Fantaisie et du Songe, which benefited from the participation of the Nabis painters and the Symbolist poets (the latter known familiarly as 'Cymbalists' because they made a great deal of noise) and which was consequently considered one of the privileged locations of the Parisian avant-garde of the time: *Ubu Roi* by Alfred Jarry was staged here in 1896.

Aurélien Lugné had added to his own the name of Poe in homage to the poet who, via Baudelaire, had left his mark on the whole of his generation, as is likewise indicated by the sign of the Chat Noir, adopted as its symbol by the artistic and literary cabaret that was regarded at that time as the 'brain of Paris'.

Satie never mentioned Poe directly in his writings, but he nevertheless implicitly recognized his influence in an autobiographical text, indicating that he 'owed much to Christopher Columbus, for the American spirit has occasionally tapped him on the shoulder and he has, with joy, its ironically icy bite'.

After having mounted — in a set by Toulouse-Lautrec — the 4th century Sanskrit drama *Mrcchakatika* ('The Little Clay Cart') in a free adaptation by Victor Barrucand, Lugné-Poe received the following letter:

Eglise Métropolitaire d'Art de Jésus conducteur
Erik Satie, Parcier & Maître de Chapelle
       to Monsieur Lugné-Poe
              Abbacy, the 24th of the month of January
                     of 1895

LUCIEN LANTIER

Sir,   on the day following the performance of *The Little Clay Cart* it is my duty, which I shall perform to the full, to protest against the literary morality represented by the theatre of which you are the impresario.

You profane art in making use of superior works which you degrade by putting them in contact with inferior and unhealthy productions; you pass off the basest things in the guise of genius, deceiving, thereby, those whom you ought to be enlightening, and by so doing you are one of the causes of the aesthetic and moral decadence of our age. You are very guilty.

The reputations cooked up in your laboratory are mendacious and pernicious: they are the result of vanity and ambition, unjustified by any sincerity. God who sees us and judges us will ask a terrible account of you for your harmful deeds; but, in the meantime, We who are conscious of our mission and who suffer and fight to accomplish it, deny you the right to speak in the name of Art, which you and those around you have trampled underfoot. Such is My protest. To reply to it would be unbecoming on your part. God, the Church and We will reply by the triumph of Art and your confusion, unless an insane blindness on your part compels Me to act ahead of time and give you the lesson you would deserve if you were to insist on pestering Me with your recriminations against the present declaration. In any case, I shall always be here to observe you and judge you.

Do not forget it.   Erik Satie

When he read this letter of excommunication — spitefully written in red ink — at a time when he was confined to bed as the result of a metal casting falling on his foot during the first performance — Lugné-Poe was somewhat impressed. But that did not prevent him from giving, on 15 March, another series of performances: four one act plays — *La Scène* by André Lebey, *Intérieur* by Maeterlinck, *La Vérité dans le vin* by Collé and *Les Pieds nickelés* by Tristan Bernard — the combination of which, as he was later to admit himself, was really not the happiest. The results of this imprudence were not long in coming.

The very next day *Le Journal des Débats* carried the following statement:

Yesterday evening at the door of the Nouveau Théâtre, where Aurélien Lugné-Poe stages interesting performances from the Oeuvre, some Gentlemen were distributing a sort of prospectus which we reproduce without changing a comma:

'Christians who wish to lodge complaints of an aesthetic nature relating to M. Lugné-Poe, the Théâtre de l'Oeuvre which he manages and the detestable Press which inspires and glorifies him, should report them to the seat of our Abbacy, 6 rue Cortot. Our brothers will find in us a rampart against the Satanic works printed in *Le Mercure de France*, *La Revue Blanche* and *La Plume*, and at the same time the energy required to assure the respect due to God, the Church and Art'.

This little announcement is signed Erik Satie and emanates, it seems, from the Eglise Métropolitaine d'Art de Jésus conducteur. We should be heartbroken to be confused with the 'detestable Press' and strongly encourage those of our brothers who have been offended by the Satanism of M. Collé, M. Maurice Maeterlinck and M. Tristan Bernard to immediately convey their grievances to the Abbacy of M. Erik Satie, aka the Rampart of the rue Cortot.

Some time later, however, the Parcier decided to show his magnanimity: in a pamphlet produced at the author's own expense, whose purpose it was to smite 'the vulgarian who injures the pure' (*Commune qui mundi nefas)*, he published the following:

Act of Clemency

In conformity with the interdiction placed upon him, M. Lugné-Poe has respectfully refrained from any reply, recrimination or complaint to the decree of the Eglise Métropolitaine d'Art de Jésus Conducteur. We are inclined to believe, without rejoicing in the fact, that in default of sincerity, the surveillance which the Church exercises over him will lead him to mend his ways and distance himself from the perverse Spirit that is all powerful over his soul and to cease the glorification of the Evil One, of whom he is one of the devotees.

By order of the Definitory
Erik Satie

Before founding this autonomous sect, Satie had filled the role of *Maître de Chapelle* to the Tiers Ordre esthétique de la Rose + Croix catholique du Temple et du Graal, founded by Sâr Péladan. Even before he met Péladan, Satie had been a great admirer of his first novel, *Le Vice suprême*.

Joseph-Aimé, known as Joséphin, Péladan described himself as 'a novelist, art critic, historian, dramatist, archaeologist and philosopher' and made no secret of his pronounced taste for ceremonial and showy dress, which was the delight of caricaturists. He was the son of the Chevalier Adrien Péladan, an associate of the Néo-Templerie de Genoude and founder of the Cult of the Wound in the Left Shoulder of Our Lord Jesus Christ, and had inherited an extraordinary library of hermetic works from his brother, Adrien Péladan Jr, who had died of poisoning by a medicine he had concocted himself.

A Erik Satie
Maître de Chapelle
LE SALON
de la Rose Croix
JOSÉPHIN PÉLADAN

Péladan

Thereby giving an example to Satie, Péladan affirmed that 'just as Religion has made itself into art in order to speak to the masses, so Art must make itself into a religion in order to speak to the minority'. It was in the course of the evenings of theatre, music and painting organized by the Sâr at the Galerie Durand Ruel, in connection with a *Salon de Peinture Rose + Croix*, that Satie first saw works of his performed in public, notably the preludes to *Le Fils des Etoiles*, a 'Wagnérie Kaldéenne' by Péladan, preludes which — doubtless without the knowledge of the latter, who knew nothing about music but was nevertheless a fanatical Wagnerian — were extremely un-Wagnerian.

The success of these evenings led to Erik Satie's name finally appearing in the press, but with the disadvantage that it was inevitably coupled with the Sâr's.

Intolerant of this confusion, Satie was led to clarify the situation by means of an open letter addressed to the regular author of the column entitled 'Propos de coulisses' in *Gil Blas* (a journalist who had borrowed his pseudonym, Gaultier Garguille, from a famous jester at the Hôtel de Bourgogne in the 16th century).

Erik Satie to M. Gaultier Garguille
Associate Editor of *Gil Blas*
Paris, the 14th of the month of August of 92
Sir,
I am greatly surprised that I,
a poor fellow who has no other thought
than of his Art, continually
have imposed upon Me the title of initiator
in music of the disciples of Monsieur
Joséphin Péladan.
This causes Me much grief and pain
For if I am to be considered anyone's pupil
I believe I can say that it is of no one
else but Myself; moreover I also believe
that Monsieur Péladan, for all his
wide learning, could not make

disciples, either in music or
    in painting or in anything else.
  Thus this good Monsieur Joséphin Péladan,
for whom I have great respect and deference,
has never exercised authority over
    the independence of My aesthetic; his
      position in relation to Me is not
that of My master but of My collaborator,
in the same way as My old friends
Messieurs J.P. Contamine de Latour
    and Albert Tinchant.
     Before Holy Mary
    mother of Our Lord Jesus, Third
      Person of the Holy Trinity:
I have said, without hatred or evil
intent, what my heart feels
in this matter; and solemnly swear
before the Fathers of the Holy Catholic
Church that I have not taken issue
in this affaire from any desire for disputation
            with My friend Monsieur Péladan.
Please accept, Sir
           the humble greetings of a
        poor fellow who has no other
      thought than of his Art, and who is
    sorry to have to deal with a subject that is so
painful to him.
      Erik Satie

In addition to the very significant assertion of 'aesthetic independence' expressed by this twenty-six-year-old composer, we must note in this letter the reference to the Virgin as 'the third person in the Holy Trinity.' Contradicting Catholic dogma — which subsumes in the one God, the Father, Son and Holy Ghost — the triad put forward by Satie seems rather to go back to the religion of ancient Egypt: Osiris, Horus, Isis. We know that Isis is hidden behind the appearance of the Virgin in many heretical sects, so much so that the belief has been expressed that the ambiguous appellation of the cathedral Notre Dame de Paris actually refers to this Egyptian goddess. According to Conrad Satie, it was while contemplating the ogives of this church for days on end that the composer conceived *Ogives*, one of his first ascetic pieces for piano. Specialists are agreed in seeing in the ogive a stylized representation of the sacred fire and in the names 'Is-is' and 'Je-sus' onomatopoeic terms conjuring up the crackling of flames.

However that may be, we must note that Satie's Epistle to the Catholic artists was published in *Le Coeur*, an esoteric periodical whose very title is a metaphor for Isis, and that at the same time Satie composed a prelude for *La Porte Héroïque du Ciel* by Jules Bois (founder and editor of *Le Coeur*), a drama in which we see Jesus in person inciting a Poet to dethrone the Virgin and replace her with Isis.

Isis' colour is white. A longing for 'whiteness' is implied in all Erik Satie's works. In his *Mémoires d'un Amnésique* Satie went so far as to assert that he lived entirely on white food: 'sugar, grated bones, salt, the mildew from fruit, cotton salad and certain fish without the skin.'

Satie was never reconciled with Péladan, who requested new scores for his *Fils des Etoiles* from other musicians, among them Edgard Varèse. A letter sent by Satie at the end of his life to an occultist writer anxious to render posthumous homage to Péladan (killed in 1918 by a tainted oyster) nevertheless shows that he was not indifferent to this contact that so deeply marked his youth.

✟

Erik Satie to Victor Emile Michelet

Sunday 23 November 1924

Dear Monsieur Victor Emile Michelet — I am desolate that occupied as I am by an insane amount of work at the Théâtre des Champs Elysées it has been impossible for me to deal with your request. I am in Paris all the time, therefore your second note did not reach me until yesterday morning (Saturday).

What can I do? . . . I would have been very happy to join the friends of Péladan, whose memory is still very dear to me.

What can I do? Please see.

Amicalement vôtre: ES

ACADEMIES

At the moment when he was preparing to break with Sâr Péladan, Satie considered the possibility of exchanging his title of Maître de Chapelle des Rose + Croix for the even more brilliant one of Academician. At this time he was twenty-six years old and most of the works he listed in his application still remained to be composed, and some of them never would be.

Erik Satie to the Secrétaire perpétuel
of the Académie des Beaux Arts

[June 1892]

Très honoré Maître,

This is to inform you that I am submitting My candidature for the seat at the Académie des Beaux Arts left vacant by the death of the late lamented Ernest Guiraud.

In soliciting the great honour of entering your illustrious Company, My ambition is not to cause the distinguished artist, whose loss is irreparable and who is irreplaceable, to be forgotten, My wish is to render a powerful affirmation of the vitality of the musical school of which I was the initiator and the artistic principles which I have always upheld in the course of my works.

In support of my candidature, très honoré Maître, I take the liberty of listing my principal works as follows:

Danses Romanes, for orchestra
Danses Gothiques
Danses Byzantines
Gymnopédies, three orchestral suites
Sarabandes
Gnossiennes, seven orchestral suites
Kharaséos, one act play
Le Fils des Etoiles, three act play (performed in 1892 at
    the Theatre of the Rose + Croix)
Le Nazaréen, three act play

I venture to request you, Monsieur le Secrétaire perpétuel, to consider this letter as a declaration of candidature, and to kindly do what is required.

In this hope,
please accept the assurances of my profound respect.

Erik Satie
6 rue Cortot

This initiative was not universally appreciated. Another candidate, Emile Pessard, a professor at the Conservatoire (at this moment teaching harmony to the young Ravel) hastened to warn one of the eminent persons who would have been called upon to vote.

Emile Pessard to an unidentified Academician

[June 1892]

[. . .] If the Institute wants a remarkable teacher, Théodore Dubois would be entirely suitable, but his dramatic works are fewer than mine, even though he is my 'senior' [. . .] Paladilhe has not composed as much as I, but he is certain to be supported by Legouvé [. . .]. Erik Satie is the musician of Sâr Péladan + Rose + Croix [. . .]. He is a complete lunatic. He has never done anything [. . .]

Emile Pessard

Twenty years later, when relating the story of his assaults on the Institut de France in his *Mémoires d'un Amnésique*, Satie wrote:

[. . .] It is always with melancholy that I shall remember M. Emile Pessard, my old sparring partner. I was able to observe, on many different occasions that he was very bad at it, devoid of all skill, lacking the simplest guile. He doesn't know, and it's only too obvious that he doesn't know. *Pauvre bon Monsieur!* What difficulty he will have in finding a place for himself, in slipping into a bosom that is so unfriendly, so inhospitable! For twenty years I've been watching him putting his back to this thankless, this surly, this sad object; while his subtle *compères* from the Palais Mazarin look at him astonished, surprised by his incompetent tenacity and his pallid impotence.

And that causes me great grief.

In 1894, when it was time to replace the late Academician Charles Gounod, Satie must have thought that his new title of 'Parcier' was bound to win him greater respect. On discovering, soon afterwards — when his candidature was rejected — that this was not at all the case, he decided to strike a dramatic blow.

As a present to himself on his twenty-eighth birthday he published the following open letter in a major musical magazine, *Le Menestrel*:

Erik Satie, Parcier et Maître de Chapelle, to M. Camille Saint-Saëns [President of the Jury]
to express My indignation and to do him a good turn

Paris, 17 May 1894

Sir,

    I offered myself to your vote to succeed M. Charles Gounod

        as a member of your Company.

        I was not yielding to an impulse of insane presumption

            but to a duty of conscience.

              A sense of justice or, failing that,

simple courtesy led Me to believe that My candidature,

    authorized by God, would be accepted by you.

    I was deeply grieved to see vulgar preferences cause you to forget solidarity in Art.

> Let those of My rivals upon whom you have committed the same outrage humiliate themselves; for My part, I remain strong in My right to be considered, if only as existent.

You can reproach Me with only one thing:

    not knowing Me as I know you.

> If I am far from you, you should not remain unaware of Me, but on the contrary, draw closer to Me.

    By judging Me from a distance and making up your mind, you have acted like an outcast and brought hell upon yourself.

Your aberration can only spring from the
weakness of your grasp on the ideas of the Century and
your misappreciation of God, the direct cause of aesthetic
debasement.

I pardon you in Jesus Christ and
embrace you in the grace of God.

Erik Satie
6 rue Cortot

A third and final letter of candidature to the Académie des
Beaux Arts was posted by Satie on the death of Ambroise
Thomas in 1896. Having failed to achieve any better
result than on his two previous attempts, he must
doubtless have felt a very particular disappointment this
time, proportionate to the pleasure he would have
experienced at sitting in the chair of the man who, as
Director of the Conservatoire, had once characterized him
as 'a very insignificant student'.

Satie consoled himself in his own way, a quarter of a
century later, by mixing extracts from Ambroise Thomas'
Mignon with fragments of Saint-Saëns' *Danse Macabre* in a
score of 'Furniture Music' — a music which was not to be
listened to.

CONTESTS

The platform of the Eglise Métropolitaine d'Art was destined also to provide Satie with the opportunity to get himself talked about in one of the most influential musical columns of the day, at a time when his work had been neither published nor performed in concert. Once only, at the Soirées Rose + Croix, in March 1892, had there been a performance of his *Préludes du 'Fils des Etoiles'*. Reporting this musical evening in the *Echo de Paris*, in which he had a regular column entitled 'La Lettre de l'Ouvreuse du Cirque d'Eté' (Letter from the Cirque d'Eté Usherette), Henry Gauthier-Villars, otherwise known as Willy, had stated that this 'faucet salesman's music' had afforded him only 'indifferent Satiesfaction'.

To reply to him, Satie waited till he too had at his disposal a periodical, the *Cartulaire* de l'Eglise Métropolitaine d'Art de Jésus conducteur, of which he was the founder, the managing editor, the only member of staff and also, no doubt, the only reader. The 'Usherette' had exalted the 'Wagnerian Word' in terms that, according to Satie befitted only God. On 2 May 1914 Satie wrote to Henry Gauthier-Villars, accusing him of blasphemy. In the next number of the *Echo de Paris* Gauthier-Villars replied, punning maliciously, and Satie returned to the attack on May 14 with a second letter which, like the first, he published immediately in his own journal.

Erik Satie, Parcier & Maître de Chapelle,
to Monsieur Gauthier-Villars
*Against the inflation of his Spirit
and for the protection of magnificent Things*
Abbacy, the 2nd of the month of May of 1895

Sir, the sacred character of Art renders the function of the critic especially delicate; you degrade this function by the inexcusable disrespect and incompetence
which you bring to its exercise. Know, by order of God, that all men of conscience condemn you for seeking to touch things that are above you, in order to tarnish them.

The demonic dragon of presumption is blinding you. You have committed blasphemy by your judgement on Wagner, who is for you the Unknown and the Infinite. For My part I can calmly curse him. My dynastic melodies, My athletic art and the asceticism of My life empower Me to do so. With these words, I command you to keep your distance from My person, in sorrow, silence and painful meditation.

Erik Satie

Erik Satie, Parcier & Maître de Chapelle,
to Monsieur Gauthier-Villars
In expression of the contempt attaching to his person
Abbacy, the 14th day of the month of May of 1895

Jealous of reputations too exalted for your lowly condition, great careers and lasting triumphs stir up the gall with which you attempt to smear everything you come near. I have spoken of Wagner and your deep ignorance; you reply by extravagant couplings of words, by what a writer less praiseworthy than praised, Victor Hugo, called the excrements of the mind.

Your breath exhales lies; from your mouth issue effrontery and indecency. Your turpitude has recoiled against you, displaying to the eyes of even the most simple-minded your unparalleled vulgarity.

What can men of the sane mind say when confronted by so much pride in the service of such petty evils? I can but ignore

the infamies of a buffoon; but I must raise My hand to strike down the oppressors of the Church and of Art, those who, like you, are devoid of all self-respect. Let those who hope to get the better of Me by abuse and terrorism know that I am resolute and fearless. Does Gauthier-Villars — that repulsive 'Cirque d'Eté Usherette', that sham histrion by the name of Willy, that union of three ignominies in one Abjection — imagine that because he is a sordid mercenary of the pen, a constant disgrace among the most degraded, I shall not dare to do to him what I would do to the worst felon?

Let him have no illusions.

Erik Satie

The unusual content of these two letters, as well as their singular presentation — headed writing paper of impressive proportions, embellished with emblems of the Church, 'grandiose' writing, black ink alternated with red — prompted Willy (as Colette, who was at that time his wife, tells us) to have them framed to decorate his office.

Quarrelsome by nature, he did not stop there. For many years the *Echo de Paris* carried extracts from hate letters which Satie continued to send Willy — privately now, since only two issues of the *Cartulaire* ever appeared — together with the merciless rejoinders that Willy took pleasure in addressing to him publicly.

If Satie called Willy an 'adulterous child of hell, made from the Devil's saliva', a 'perfidious blasphemer', an 'impudent *brucolaque*', or a 'dull-witted pen-pusher', 'a dumb and spineless simpleton and a dreary piece of literary garbage', Willy described Satie as an 'anagogical wash-out', an 'esoteric slut', an 'inSatieable mystic', a 'penniless street musician who bangs the big drum', a 'Debussy who passed through Charenton' — Charenton being the name of a madhouse famous, among other things, for having harboured the Marquis de Sade.

Satie and Willy went as far as physical assault. On Sunday 10 April 1904, Ricardo Viñes notes in his unpublished diary: 'In the afternoon I went to the last of the Chevillard concerts, where Willy struck Erik Satie with his cane after Satie had intentionally thrown Willy's hat on the floor. The city police took Satie away.'

We can clearly picture the scene between the small, malicious Satie and the large Willy furious at the outrage committed against his elegant flat-brimmed top-hat. In any case, as in a Chaplin film, it was the little man who was led away between two policemen: the important personage, even though he had been the one to strike the blow, was treated with deference.

Nevertheless, the long quarrel between Satie and Willy was to have an unexpected epilogue. Ten years after this 'walking-stick duel' the Countess de Chabannes invited Erik Satie to a gathering to which three of Satie's 'faithful enemies' had also been invited: the critics Jean Marnold, Louis Laloy and Willy. The Countess de Chabannes, née Armande de Polignac, had met Satie at the Schola Cantorum. She herself was well thought of as a composer and an orchestra leader.

After the reception, the Countess received the following letter of thanks: .

Erik Satie to the Countess de Chabannes

Arcueil, 3 June 1914

Madame,

I must tell you how much I enjoyed being in the company of my ferocious enemies.

These terrible individuals crushed, mummified, plastered, petrified, buried, defeathered and shrank me.

I came home in the Metro *alone* with Willy. Yes, Madame. And I can tell you that after a Corsican contest lasting twenty-two years, it was with a pounding heart that I shook hands with this good man!

Therefore, Madame, I wish to thank you for the exquisite moments over which you so delightfully presided.

And I ask you to give my best regards to Monsieur de Chabannes and to see in me the respectful

ES

HOMES

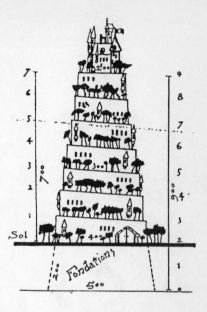

The Eglise Métropolitaine d'Art de Jésus Conducteur had made itself much talked about, even if not for precisely ecclesiastical reasons. If we are to believe this brief note addressed to the *Intermédiaire des Chercheurs et des Curieux* (whose motto was 'seek and ye shall find, we must help one another'), interest in this institution was actually on the increase.

Eglise Métropolitaine d'Art. A short while ago I saw some printed matter emanating from the Eglise Métropolitaine d'Art de Jésus Conducteur, signed with the name Erik Satie, Parcier and Maître de Chapelle, 6 rue Cortot. I wish to know: what is this Montmartre institution?

César Birotteau

We have, however, good reason to question the true identity of the signatory of this note, César Birotteau being the name of one of Balzac's characters who, after a brief period of prosperity, was ruined.

In the course of the year 1895, fortified by a mysterious 'inheritance', Satie had assumed the considerable expenses demanded by the prestige of his role as Parcier: costly notepaper bearing a letterhead designed by himself, the printing of an independent publication, the *Cartulaire*, as well as new clothes. Oddly enough, the Parcier of the Eglise Métropolitaine d'Art had abandoned the long gown which he had worn for some years previously, and which gave him something of the appearance of a priest. For the next seven years he wore a suit of velvet corduroy — in the style of the Montmartre painters — of which he had bought seven identical sets, with coat and hat to match. Nicknamed *the Velvet Gentleman*, he kept open table for his many friends in one of the best restaurants of Montmartre.

This prosperity was to prove short-lived. One day Conrad Satie, an engineer specializing in the chemistry of perfumes, received the following appeal, addressed — no doubt in order the better to play on his feelings — to 'Tiby'. 'Tiby' and 'Pouillot' were the two nicknames Erik had given his brother when they were children.

Erik Satie to Conrad Satie

[12 July 1896?]

My poor Tiby, I am ruined. The wheel of fortune is no longer in My grasp; it is destitution; that woman with the huge breasts who has come to keep Me company from now on.

What will you say?

My evident wish to tell you of My fall, yesterday, in front of our friends. I don't know what prevented Me from doing so; no doubt My memory failed Me, that often happens; or something stopped Me; a trifle sometimes makes us leave undone what we most wanted to do; and then, perhaps, I noticed that it was not the right moment; that it might have been looked at askance, or that your reply might have been cold. Yes: I am ruined.

What will you say?

The most troublesome part of it is over; unfortunately I haven't a sou in my purse, that's the worst thing. It would be very kind if you would send Me a little help in the shape of a money order; without which I shall be exposed to cruel suffering, I tell you. After all, you may say, that serves him right; he shouldn't have spent his money so fast. I know. The 'Cupboard' is waiting to receive Me in three days: I'm

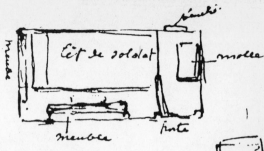

planning to move house next quarter; I've already given notice.

I'm counting on you to provide a haven for My cherished possessions; My portrait by de Feure, the one by La Rochefoucauld and many drawings. In addition there are a table, two benches and a coffer.

What will you say?

I embrace you and beg you to forgive Me for what I have done.

Erik Satie

It was no doubt with this move in prospect that Satie sent himself the following letter, signed with the emblem of his Church, a Greek cross and a Latin cross linked, possibly symbolizing the Catholic and oriental faiths which he planned to reconcile.

Erik Satie to Erik Satie

Paris, the 14th day of the month of July of 1896
Tomorrow will be the day, Messire.

Humbly

The following day he left the room — itself not particularly confortable — which till then he had occupied (at a rent of 35.10 fr. a quarter) on the top floor at 6 rue Cortot and moved into an even cheaper closet on the ground floor. In this 'cupboard' there was no room to stand up. The bed functioned — according to the time of day — as an altar or as a work table. Satie also designed many castles, his ideal homes, on this 'table'. . .

Two years later Satie, who had 'so many ideas to house',
decided to move to the suburbs where rents were lower.
He found in the house known as the Maison des Quatre
Cheminées at 22 rue Cauchy in Arcueil — the birthplace
of one of his closest friends of this period, Henry Pacory —
a room that was quite spacious although devoid of all
conveniences. The tenant who preceded him in the
Quatre Cheminées was Bibi la Purée, a 'clochard' related
to Rodolphe Salis, the director of the Chat Noir, and very
popular in the Quartier latin. His portrait was painted by
Steinlen and by Picasso.

When he went to rent this room, Satie had asked Henry
Pacory and their mutual friend, the painter Grass-Mick,
to accompany him. Grass-Mick described the scene later
in his unpublished memoirs: 'In ten minutes the rental
was arranged. Satie had a new home. If three or four
friends, including his brother Conrad, entered his room
after his death, no one ever set foot in it during his lifetime.
Consequently, if Pacory is still alive, he and I are the only
people ever to have seen this room, the first and the last,
for, once Satie had moved in, it was to close the door on the
world outside. Who would have thought it, seeing this
man who in himself was so correct? Here was a dwelling
which he occupied for twenty-seven years and which
wasn't to be known to even ten people. Pacory and I saw it
bare, the others rummaged through it. That was all.'

None of Satie's friends who forced the door after his death will ever forget the effect made upon them by the jumble of heterogeneous objects that met their eyes. According to Jean Wiéner it looked like an immense spider's web. Robert Caby said he felt as if he were stepping into the composer's brain.

Conrad Satie was not offended at not being allowed into the Maison des Quatre Cheminées during his brother's lifetime. 'I'm just the same at home,' he wrote in his notebook. 'Visits from friends break my imaginary toys and muddle my thoughts that are piled up in the corners in apparent disorder.'

Playing as always the same role in relation to Erik that Theo Van Gogh played with regard to his brother Vincent, it was Conrad again who helped him with the move materially. Satie kept him regularly informed of the various stages in setting up house.

Erik Satie to Conrad Satie

Arcueil, the 9th of the month of October of 98
I spent the night from Friday to Saturday at Arcueil: mosquitoes, certainly sent by the Freemasons, came to visit me and deigned to bite me all over; probably because they found me tasty, but certainly because I had left open the window that looks out on the countryside, the only window there is, by the way [. . .]

Arcueil, the 8th of the month of November of 98
I'm here now to rub down the floor of my room with washing soda and anoint it with soft soap; when this task is completed I shall wax the aforesaid floor myself [. . .]

Arcueil, the 21st of the month of November of 1898
You ask me for an official list of the expenditures required by the move to Arcueil? There is the Arcueil rent — 25 fr 50 — plus a modest day's wage for the man who is kind

enough to assist me in this situation, because I shall be compelled to have recourse to the services of someone of this type. This month of December will suffice me to move a major part of the so-called valuable articles. Unfortunately, as I pointed out above, the various planks, the mattress, the chest and the bench will have to be carried by a hand-barrow [. . .]

Arcueil, the 22nd of the month of January of 99
My good Pouillot, My home is perfectly adequate, there's plenty of space. In front of me I see a cottage belonging to a Lord of the region who practises the profession of master mason. This modest workman, who has been able to save up a few pence and a great many more shillings without being taught how to, is the father of a young Miss who is as dignified and pretty as a Lady.

Poor little baby! Don't imagine not even for one hour* that I am in love with her, seeing that I care no more about her father the Lord, her or the Missus, her dear mother, than about the tooth that caused me so much pain, you remember when. As far as her dear mother is concerned, it seems she passed away close on two years ago.

So I can absolutely disregard the latter. No one can object or ever know anything about it.

In a public house of this town I made the acquaintance of an old gentleman who is educated to the tips of the fingers of his two hands and the toes of his two feet. Although he wears woollen socks and always has his hands in his pockets, his education catches your eye and amazes you.

As soon as he saw me, he said:

'Do you know that the law is infamous in its way? I defy anyone to take away one hair from my head, because . . . I haven't any. Anyway, I'd rather have no hair at all than ugly hair: because it's better to inspire envy than pity.

'I don't like cats and dogs; I look upon them as insects. Isn't it true that if you put a cat in a dark room it gives off sparks as soon as you stroke its fur? What a way to behave! Well, Monsieur, it would be difficult to do as much to lots of

Monsieur Sadi dans sa maison
Il songe

people. If the dog has a tail it is simply to enable him to laugh in society, just like you and me, or perhaps so that people can tread on it from time to time, just to change the habit of treading on its paws, something that happens quite often, since God intentionally puts it under the feet of poor people. As for women, they are venomous, crawling snakes; every-one knows, or doesn't know, that they bite treacherously, suck your blood and crush your chest, especially if they are very heavy, of course.'

And he went on for a long time in this vein.

* As to the hour, note, it's one o'clock; moreover it's Sunday, and I haven't had a letter from you, my big Pouillot. Watch out for the Scorpions.

Arcueil, the 5th of the month of February of 99
Monsieur Pouillot,

May the Lord be with Pouillot. . . . May the Sacred Name of God and that venerated by the Great Definitor act blissfully upon Our weak spirits and may they be found at the same time in all truly Christian mouths. Hallelujah!

I am very glad to be in Arcueil. I do not forget that I owe it to you. The environs, including Gentilly, are so sad, so tearful that it moves Me and is as agreeable to Me as a badly dressed, pale and pretty wolf, the good one.

How gentle, pitiable and grandiose all the people are! And in this out-of-the-way corner you can sense the mysterious dwelling-place of Notre Dame Bassesse, Our Lady Lowliness, this person who is almost divine, or perhaps even more than divine. Death, our little Sister, the one you talk about with such joy, must love these suburbs all so filled with herself. At each step, you see, you meet phantoms assuming a human or animal appearance, no doubt in order to be more funny.

In any case, whether they are humans or whether they are animals, they know how to make you forget that they exist in the most elegant possible way.

A country of peace and hatred, because it is cursed in advance it makes a deep impression; and people say under their breath that it is a knight of St George cast out of the Order for having had unnatural relations with an excommunicate.

Erik Satie

Living in Arcueil was not more comfortable than living in Montmartre. Conrad was able to note that his brother's relationship with God was progressively deteriorating as his material situation grew worse.

Arcueil, the 14th of the month of April of 99
Monsieur Pouillot,
Why attack God himself? He is just as unhappy as we could be; since the death of his poor son he has no taste for anything and only nibbles at his food.

Although he has seated him on his good old right hand, he is still completely flabbergasted that men could play such a nasty trick on the one he cherished; and he only has time to murmur, in the saddest way possible, that wasn't fair!

I doubt whether at this moment he would send down to earth even one of his nephews; mankind has changed his mind about sending members of his family out on trips.

Let's leave him in peace, My friends; let us pray to him sincerely, as of course we ought to do.

It is I, Saint Erik of Arcueil, Parcier and Martyr, who tells it to you.

Arcueil, the 22nd of the month of July of 99
[. . .] since you know my piety towards the Lord. There's no sense in him bothering to test Me; the mortifications I inflict on Myself are enough, he ought to know that, and I don't see why I should always have him between My feet or on My back stupidly watching what I'm doing [. . .]

[December 1899]

It was a good idea of yours to send me that little present; it wasn't put into a haversack, but straight into my pocket, where it didn't stay long. If the dead go fast, money, which is no more stupid than anything else, goes equally fast; and it's a pleasure to see it walk straight ahead without looking round, and as proud as punch as it goes. I think men are not so much liars as they are stupid. Watching them run after each other, the Wise Man has to leave them without a murmur. An incautious word would spoil the spectacle which these ladies and gentlemen present to us every day; and then where would we spend our gala evenings [. . .] I'm beginning to believe that the Good Lord is a dirty old man the kind of which there aren't many. His supposed mercy — I can see he hides it somewhere and draws it out very rarely.

Shall I tell you what I think? That's not going to bring him happiness and it wouldn't surprise me if he ended up losing his job. And a good thing too [. . .]

Arcueil, the 7th of the month of June of 1900

I'm dying of boredom: everything I begin timidly fails with a certainty I've never before known till now.

What can I do but turn towards God and point the finger at him? I end up thinking the old man is even more stupid than powerful.

What's new with you? Tell me, old chap; your future isn't the same as mine, fortunately for you; you'll have a horse and one of those big carriages that's open in summer and closed in winter and you'll be driving off all over the place the way moneyed people do.

I clasp you in my poor arms

Erik Satie

Towards the end of his life Satie's relations with God improved. Meeting Stravinsky in the street one day, he confided in him: 'I went to a bit of Communion this morning.' On Good Friday 1925 — the last year of his life — Jacques Maritain is said to have heard him reply to the

Erik SATIE peint par
lui-même, avec une pensée:
« Je suis venu au monde très
jeune dans un temps très vieux. »

Erik SATIE
Par lui-même

Etude pour un buste
de M. Erik SATIE
peint par lui-même,
Je suis venu au monde
très jeune dans un temps
très vieux.

Projet pour un
buste de M.
Erik SATIE
(peint par lui-même),
avec une pensée:
« Je suis venu au monde
très jeune dans un
temps très vieux. »

almoner at St Joseph's Hospital, who was inviting him to take the Easter Sacrament: 'Of course I will, I'm a Catholic.' However, that same evening, he is supposed to have said to Robert Caby: 'This morning I swallowed a wafer.' However that may be, unlike his father, an out and out atheist, he left no instructions forbidding the presence of a priest at his funeral. It was in the Arcueil cemetery that Satie was buried. A cross carved in a block of stone was the only ornament on his grave.

The Maison des Quatre Cheminées was the first of his homes to receive a commemorative plaque, on 30 June 1929.

A bust of the composer was erected in 1950 in a park of Arcueil, only to vanish shortly afterwards. The bust pedestal, engraved with his name *Erik Satie*, still exists. There was also a small blind alley in Arcueil, later demolished, named *Impasse Erik Satie*.

At the present time, there is no street in Paris named for Satie. In Honfleur a square, closed off by an iron railing, was recently named after him.

WALTZES

Although he had settled in Arcueil, Satie continued to haunt Montmartre, right up until the time when the artistic and literary centre of the capital moved from the north to the south, from Montmartre to Montparnasse. Since Arcueil lies to the south of Paris, Satie himself contributed to the move.

After the closing down of the Eglise Métropolitaine as a result of his departure, the former Parcier discovered another source of interest on the Butte, although in an entirely different domain: the café-concert.

This contact with popular music was to prove fruitful for the future evolution of his work. For the time being he lived by this experience in the most direct manner possible, since he was able to make a little bit of money as a piano accompanist — a 'tapeur à gages', as it is called in the slang of Montmartre — for an old companion from the Chat Noir, Vincent Hyspa. He wrote several tunes for the latter and composed incidental music for a pantomime devised by another pillar of Montmartre, the writer and illustrator of humorous magazines, Jules Dépaquit. The English title of this pantomime — *Jack in the Box* — testified to the Anglophilia of French intellectuals at this period, which ultimately led to the Entente Cordiale.

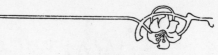

Erik Satie to Conrad Satie

Arcueil, the 14th of the month of March of 99
[. . .] As a result of being offered work of extreme lowliness
(accompaniment), I have wasted valuable time but earned
some money from this trade. It's old Hyspa I've been
accompanying during several evening performances. Your
coat, your good old shirts made this little game possible for
me [. . .]

Erik Satie

Erik Satie to Conrad Satie

[Monday 3 April 1899]
It's four o'clock and we've reached Monday 3. Has the
letter got lost? I'm very worried. I haven't eaten for two days
[. . .]

Arcueil, the 15th of the month of May of 99
My good Pouillot,
   All this is no fun: for my part I'm getting completely fed up
with it: an empty stomach, a parched throat, give me no
pleasure whatsoever. I'd like to say that right away.
   Exhaustion and anaemia, I see poverty, that old bitch,
giving birth to one endless series of monstrosities whereas a
childish calculation, and most calculations are childish, by
the way, shows me most pleasantly, with fine precision, that
all these things will turn out disastrously for me, perhaps for
everyone.
   I have been able to observe, and I continue to do so every
day, that I am very badly affected and that, against my will, I
shall have to lay down my arms quicker than I would wish.

My mind is growing more and more confused, I'm getting close to decrepitude for a young man; not that I give a damn. It's more than I need [. . .]

Ton vieux frère

P.S. Note to the addressee: I'm working with Dépaquit on a pantomime that is to go to the Comédie Parisienne next October. Details follow.

4 July 1899

[. . .] As for my 'cloonerie', it's more of a 'cloonerie' than a pantomime, I'm expecting a flop of magnificent proportions: remove, please, all doubts about it. Did I tell you the title?

Jack in the Box, that's the title. I'm very glad to be working on it, this knock-about turn consoles me a little and will be my way of cocking a snook at the wicked men who people our world [. . .] Erik Satie

Satie did not succeed in getting *Jack in the Box* performed during his lifetime. The only compositions of this period to be played in public were a few music-hall songs sung by Paulette Darty and Vincent Hyspa. Darty, known at the time as 'the Queen of the Slow Waltz', has recalled their first meeting:

> Usually I received composers in the morning who came to present their new tunes to me.
>
> That morning I was resting when an unfamiliar name was announced, 'Monsieur Erik Satie'. My secretary saw him. He was accompanied by M. Bellon, a music publisher, who had a very nice voice.
>
> So suddenly I heard the waltz *Je te veux* (now famous). Satie had simply installed himself at the piano and M. Bellon sang. It was so particularly charming, and so pretty that I hastily slipped on a dressing gown and went to tell Monsieur Satie how delighted I was. He sat down again at the piano and I sang *Je te veux* for the first time . . . Since then I have sung *Je te veux*, *Tendrement*, and that delightful song *La Diva de*

'*L'Empire*', all over the place with enormous success [. . .] Oh, no one could be bored when Satie came to the house for a family meal. What an unforgettable man! He really was an ace.

Satie remained her friend even after Paulette Darty had left the stage to marry the lace manufacturer Edouard Dreyfus. She introduced Satie to her former patron, Maurice de Féraudy, an actor and artistic director at the Comédie Française, who had written a play in collaboration with a certain Jean Kolb. The title of this play, for which Satie was to write incidental music, was *Pousse l'Amour*, the name of an old aphrodisiac drink which the editors of the *Festin d'Esope*, Apollinaire's magazine, had restored 'to honour and use.'

In connection with this play too, Satie encountered the usual difficulties.

Erik Satie to Paulette Darty

Arcueil, 6 January 1907

Ma bonne Amie,

It is trembling with emotion that I take up my pen to timidly wish a Happy New Year to you and to the good Monsieur Dreyfus.

What's new?

A strange thing happened to me in Wednesday at the théâtre des Capucines. Monsieur de Féraudy got angry with the theatre manager during the rehearsal of our little play. Can you guess why?

So our little play, you might say, is at the bottom of a canal and will stay there for a long while, since no one is going to look for it. Poor me!

And people will say I'm lucky!

It's enough to make you die laughing. Nothing like it ever happened before, not even in the comics.

I'll come and tell you about it one of these days: you'll split your sides.

I send you my good wishes several times over and beg you to give my regards to Monsieur Dreyfus.

ES

Nevertheless *Pousse l'Amour* was staged, on 22 November 1907, at another theatre, the Comédie Royale, then revived in Monte Carlo on 28 February 1913, but in the form of an operetta and under a new title, *Coco chéri*. Libretto and music are now lost.

As to Paulette Darty, having lost touch with her for some years, Satie met her one evening at the house of a mutual friend. The poet Blaise Cendrars was there as well and reminisced about the meeting during a French radio broadcast in 1950. Finding her again 'Satie, overcome by emotion, went to the piano and played the two waltzes, the *valse chaloupée* and a song he had originally composed for her, but whose title I forget. Paulette Darty was a very nice woman, not exactly the youngest nor the sveltest when I knew her, she had put on some excess weight, but she had a divine laugh, a joyous laugh . . . extremely young. She sang, and then Satie took her on his lap and they played a four-handed piece that they must have been improvising on the spot, I suppose . . .'.

SOCIAL LIFE

To earn a living, Satie continued to furnish the café-concert and the music-hall with what he called 'very dirty works', even while he was studiously attending the Schola Cantorum.

And it was as a composer of light music that he introduced himself in Arcueil-Cachan when, after several years of solitary seclusion, he decided to play a part in the life of this community.

The better to play the game of social life like everyone else, he had exchanged his velvet suit for a kind of minor civil servant's uniform: bowler hat, dark suit, high wing collar, walking-stick or umbrella. Being in possession of his diploma as a Contrapuntist, he did not disdain to accept other equally conventional distinctions, such as honorific title of an Officier d'Académie, on 4 July 1909, for services to his fellow citizens.

He had begun by organizing *Matinées Artistiques* for the Cercle Lyrique et Théâtral of Arcueil-Cachan. His contacts in the variety theatre had enabled him to attract stars to the humble assembly hall of this suburban municipality.

Erik Satie to Vincent Hyspa

Arcueil, 22 October 1909

Cher Monsieur,
      I say to you:
Don't forget your music. Come by the noon train, 2, gare du
Luxembourg. Don't be late, will you?
  Come with your lady.
  Bring M. Dépaquit too.
  Take care, I beg you.
I squeeze the tips of your fingers to make you cry.

ES

Invited to the same matinée performance, Paulette Darty
'literally brought the house down with applause'. Of course
she sang Erik Satie's songs.
    The newspaper *L'Avenir d'Arcueil-Cachan* warmly sup-
ported these events, and for a very good reason. The
anonymous supplier of these accounts, who also recorded
with great wit other local events, was none other than Erik
Satie. Humbly Satie submitted his reviews every two weeks
to the editor of the paper, the architect Pierre Alexandre
Templier, who was the father of his future biographer,
Pierre Daniel Templier.

Erik Satie to Pierre Alexandre Templier
Editor of *L'Avenir d'Arcueil-Cachan*

Arcueil, 13 September 1909

Cher Monsieur Templier,

Herewith my article. I see no need to make cuts. Have a look for yourself, please.

Amicalement votre: ES

Templier's newspaper was Radical Socialist in tendency. Anxious to identify as closely as possible with the community to which he had chosen to belong, Satie also joined this party. After the assassination of Jean Jaurès on 31 July 1914, he demonstrated his grief and indignation by leaving the Radical Party and joining the Socialist Party which Jaurès had founded. In 1921, when this party split, he chose the most extremist camp.

His neighbour and friend, the house-painter Léon Louis Veyssière, who was a Socialist of much longer standing than Satie, tried to restrain him. He received the following response.

Erik Satie to Léon Louis Veyssière

Friday 8 January 1921

Mon cher Ami —

I am an old Bolshevik & cannot join your camp. I love you just the same and hope we shall not quarrel over this.

Bien à vous

Erik Satie

At the same period he took delight in introducing himself to high society as 'Erik Satie of the Arcueil Soviet'. However, a pencilled note states that he had to give up the idea of having a musical chronicle in *L'Humanité* (the newspaper founded by Jaurès, later to become the organ of the French Communist Party) because his 'Communist friends are disconcertingly bourgeois in matters of Art'. No one was ever to see him as an 'activist', but the news of Lenin's death, which came to him in the *métro*, brought tears to his eyes.

During these years in which he took pleasure in maintaining close contact with the people of Arcueil, Satie enthusiastically took part in the founding of several societies: among others the Amis du Vieux Arcueil, for the study and preservation of ancient buildings, and a Groupe Normand, the aim of which was to reunite those who had been born in that region and whom 'the hazards of life have taken far from their native soil', but which called with equal warmth upon those from Maine, Poitou and also from Canada (a country discovered by a navigator who had set sail from Honfleur), no doubt in order to demonstrate their broad-mindedness.

However, the Arcueil association to which Satie devoted himself most assiduously was the Patronage laïque or lay charitable organization, in which he had claimed for himself the modest post of 'superintendent'. In this capacity he gave sol-fa lessons to children on Sunday mornings and on Thursday afternoons took whole classes on outings. During the summer of 1910 he even set about raising funds to enable a greater number of children — preferably those whom he had chosen himself individually — to take advantage of an outing sponsored by the mayor's office.

Erik Satie to Louis Grégoire Veyssière
    Mayor of Arcueil-Cachan

Arcueil-Cachan, 4 August 1910

Monsieur le Maire,

As in previous years, the Municipality of Arcueil-Cachan is organizing an outing for children in the summer school. The resources at the disposal of the Mayor's Office make it necessary to limit the number of children taking part in this enjoyable trip.

With the aim of obviating, so far as possible, this regrettable state of affairs, I have been able to collect from among my acquaintances a sum which makes it possible for me to enable a number of children — a dozen, six girls and six boys — to take part in a pleasure that is rarely open to them.

I ask you, Monsieur le Maire, if you will kindly permit my taking with me these dozen children I have chosen.

I enclose herewith the list of names of these children so that the ladies and gentlemen of the committee shall not include them among those they designate themselves.

Provided with the authority of the parents concerned, I will take entire responsibility for the supervision and conduct of the children who are kindly entrusted to me.

Please accept, Monsieur le Maire, my respectful salutations

Erik Satie

In reporting this 'magnificent' outing, the local paper stated that the *Satie Group* would be formed every year.

In fact this experiment was never to be repeated. In any case this group, composed exclusively of small children, was the only one to which Satie was ever willing to lend his name.

YOUNG MUSICIANS

Satie left Arcueil and its children when the possibility of re-entering the musical world of Paris and presenting not just his popular songs but all the rest of his music was offered to him by Ravel and the 'Jeunes Ravêlites.'

He had first met Ravel in the early nineties, when the latter was only a young boy accompanying his father, the engineer-inventor Joseph Ravel, to the Nouvelle Athènes Café. It was after hearing Satie's *Sarabandes*, dating from 1887, and under its influence that Ravel composed his first score, *Le Ballade de la Reine morte d'aimer* (1893).

Twenty years later, when he was spending most of his time in voluntary exile in Arcueil, Satie was surprised to see himself called back to Paris by the young man from the past, who had meanwhile become a famous composer and who now had a group of faithful followers. Shortly afterwards these young musicians and musicologists who were known as the 'Jeunes Ravêlites', organized a concert of works by Erik Satie at the Salle Gaveau. The composer was introduced as 'a brilliant precursor . . . a disturbing inventor of neologisms who, a quarter of a century ago, was already speaking the daring musical language of tomorrow.'

Satie was astonished by this sudden enthusiasm.

Erik Satie to Conrad Satie

Arcueil, 14 Jannuary 1911

Mon bon Pouillot —

Here is a programme from les Jeunes. You will see a (very incomplete) note on your old brother.

How are you?

Ravel is a Prix de Rome of very great talent; another Debussy, but more striking.

He assures me — every time I meet him — that he owes me a great deal.

If he says so.

Your brother: ES

However, as the movement grew, Satie became increasingly worried about it, to such an extent that when Jules Ecorcheville, Editor of the revue de la S.I.M. (the Société Internationale de Musique, which was closely connected, and not merely by its initials, with the S.M.I., the Société Musicale Indépendante founded by Ravel), organized an evening in his honour, he was so deeply moved that he was unable to be present.

Or had he merely used this as an excuse because he had nothing suitable to wear?

Erik Satie to Maurice Ravel

Arcueil, 4 March 1911

Mon bon Ravel,

I am writing to Monsieur Ecorcheville to say that, to my great regret, I can't come and listen to you this evening. It would be too moving and beyond my strength.

I am asking Monsieur Lerolle to act as my representative and on this occasion give my compliments to my excellent interpreters, who are marvellous.

Thank you, mon bon, for your friendly devotion.

Debussy will conduct the *Gymnopédies* on the 25th of this month at the Salle Gaveau as part of the Concert of Cercle Musical.

That's something I owe to you.

Thank you. Please give my regards to your mother.

Amicalement: ES

However, as he began to realize little by little that he was being used for purposes that were quite alien to him and, above all that, musically speaking, he had nothing in common with him, Satie set about detaching himself from Ravel.

Ravel's military aspirations during the war (he had insisted on volunteering after being retired from service), and his refusal, a little later, of the *Légion d'Honneur* ('but all his music accepts it!' remarked Satie), found no favour in his eyes. And when asked to write an article for a British review on the man who, all things considered, had been his benefactor, he hurried to make clear what the tone of the article would be, to avoid all misunderstanding.

Erik Satie to Georges Jean-Aubry

Arcueil-Cachan, 19 Nov. 1919

Mon cher Ami — I ask nothing better than to write an article on Ravel, but . . . this article may not be very much to your taste. The fault lies entirely with the deplorable and outmoded aesthetic professed by our friend. It would be difficult for me to water down what my thinking dictates. I love Ravel deeply, but his art leaves me cold, alas!

Can I write this article? You see, dear friend: I am entirely at your disposal.

Bonjour, mon cher Aubry. A bientôt

Erik Satie

Satie owed to Ravel the enjoyment of finding himself supported by the younger generation. He was often to experience this enjoyment in the course of his life.

Before the 1914 war he had at his side not merely an organized group such as the Jeunes Ravêlites (whom he preferred to call simply 'Jeunes' — the Young Ones), but

also isolated young musicians like Roland Manuel and Georges Auric. His friendship with both of them was to end unhappily ten years later.

Satie met Roland Manuel at Paulette Darty's in 1911 and immediately considered him his bosom friend. He helped him get into the Schola and introduced him to Ravel the first biographer of whom he was to become.

Satie's first meeting with Georges Auric was particularly striking.

One day in December 1913, when he had not yet become quite used to receiving compliments, Satie was surprised to come across an article praising his work in the *Revue française de Musique*. He hastened to thank the author, whose name he was reading for the first time.

Erik Satie to Georges Auric

[December 1913]

Cher Monsieur,

I read your article which is much too beautiful and which is a veritable study. I should like to meet you to thank you for it.

Suggest a date on which it would be possible for you to see me and I shall come at once [. . .]

Erik Satie

How great was the composer's surprise when, on responding to the lunch invitation which his correspondent had promptly extended to him, he discovered that 'Monsieur Auric' was a boy of fourteen, a kind of child prodigy in music criticism who, moreover, was a talented composer.

He immediately arranged for a concert in which his own works and those of little Auric alternated, and for a long time he regarded this boy as the most promising of all his young friends and the one closest to him.

After *Parade*, when Satie was in conflict with malicious critics and a public that thought it was being made fun of,

Auric and two of his friends, Louis Durey and Arthur Honegger, organized a concert at the Salle Huyghens in Montparnasse, as an homage to him. Shortly afterwards, a young woman musician, Germaine Tailleferre ('our Marie Laurencin', Satie called her, alluding to the only woman admitted by Apollinaire among the Cubist painters) joined the three others to officially form a group of which Satie liked to consider himself the fifth member. Remembering the support he had received from the 'Jeunes' before the war, he called the new group the 'Nouveaux Jeunes'.

The singer Jane Bathori, who at this time was running the Vieux Colombier, at once invited the five to perform their works. Because of their affinity with the five, the works of two other unknown young musicians were also played at these concerts: Francis Poulenc and Darius Milhaud.

Satie had corresponded with Poulenc even before meeting him.

In 1915, when he was fifteen and still attending the Conservatoire, Poulenc had had the idea of conducting an enquiry into what some of the 'well-known' French musicians thought of César Franck. Debussy, who at this period was signing himself Claude de France, informed him that, despite his esteem for the 'great Flemish musician', he did not consider it suitable for French people in time of war to concern themselves with anything other than the cultural tradition of their own country. The tone of Satie's reply was entirely different.

Erik Satie to Francis Poulenc

[October 1915]

Monsieur,

Everything leads me to suppose that Franck was a huge musician. His work is astonishingly Franckist, in the best sense of the word.

A great Paris publisher claims that Franck was lazy.

— Oui, Monsieur.

If that is true, Franck was very blameworthy, since laziness is a very nasty thing, not to be recommended, especially in a worker.

This opinion is entirely personal and in no way binding.

Please accept, Sir, the amiable amiabilities of him who is

Erik Satie

P.S. I am not 'well-known': I am a 'young quinquagenarian'.

After receiving this letter, Poulenc let the matter drop. But a little later, after the *Parade* sensation, he begged his private piano tutor, Ricardo Viñes, to introduce the composer of this ballet to him. To begin with, Satie proved rather suspicious of this scion of a great family (owners of the Rhone-Poulenc chemical factories). But an incident arising from Poulenc's ambitions brought them together.

Impatient to make his mark, the young Poulenc knocked at every door. Thus he had obtained an introduction to Paul Vidal, the incumbent conductor of the Opéra Comique and a professor of harmony of the old school.

In order to make a better impression Poulenc had brought with him his latest composition, dedicated to Erik Satie, a vocal work, *Rhapsodie nègre*, inspired by a Madagascan poem, 'Honoloulou' signed Makoko Kangourou but no doubt the work of a Parisian hoaxer. The result of this meeting was so disastrous that he felt the urgent need to unburden himself to his friend and teacher.

Francis Poulenc to Ricardo Viñes
Very urgent

26 September 1917

Mon bon cher Maître,

Something so regrettable and stupid happened to me yesterday that I want to tell you about it and ask your advice.

On the recommendation of one of my friends, who is himself a good friend of Paul Vidal, I went to see the latter to talk to him about my entry into the Conservatoire.

At the beginning of my visit he was very friendly, asking me what teachers I had had up to now and so on. . . Then I handed him the manuscript of my *Rhapsodie nègre*. He read it attentively, wrinkled his forehead, rolled his eyes furiously on seeing the dedication to Erik Satie, stood up and yelled at me exactly these words: 'Your work stinks, it is idiotic, a load of crap. You're making fun of me, fifths all over the place, and what the hell's this 'Honoloulou'? Ah! I see you're one of the gang of Stravinsky, Satie & Co., very well, goodnight!' and he almost threw me out of the house. So there I was on the pavement, not knowing what to do, whom to consult and so on. . . This incident has so upset my plans that I very much need you and your advice, I assure you.

Recevez mes amitiés

Francis Poulenc

It was Satie who replied, instead of Viñes.

Erik Satie to Francis Poulenc

Saturday, 29 September 1917

Cher Ami — I should like to see you. You seem to me to be lost, but easy to find. Fix a time and place to meet.

Who is giving you such odd advice? It's funny.

Never get mixed up with 'schools': there's been an explosion — quite natural, by the way. And then, in order to give you useful advice, I need to know what you are planning to do and capable of doing.

Your visit to Vidal was that of an *amateur pupil*, not of an *artist pupil*. He showed you that. He's one of the old school and he intimidated you.

Laugh, mon bon.

Tout à vous: ES

At the beginning of 1919 Darius Milhaud came back from Brazil, where he had been employed as secretary by the writer-diplomat Paul Claudel. Milhaud's works had been played in his absence at the Salle Huyghens and the Vieux Colombier, thanks to the devotion of his former

1915

RUE GAILLARD

fellow-student at the Conservatoire, Arthur Honegger. Without having yet met him personally, Satie had been intrigued by Milhaud's music many years earlier, when he heard it being played from the windows of a house next door to one where he frequently went to lunch with friends — a further proof, if proof were needed, of his openmindedness and untiring curiosity.

What attracted Satie later, talent apart, was Milhaud's kindness and wisdom. For his part Milhaud never forgot the moral rigour of Erik Satie, from whom, however, he remained quite far removed musically speaking.

Of all his young friends, Milhaud was the only one with whom Satie never quarrelled. It was to Milhaud, after his brother's death, that Conrad Satie entrusted his unpublished works so that he could decide where they should go.

Erik Satie to Pierre Bertin

Arcueil, 26 June 1919

Cher Ami — Thank you for your kind letter. See you Monday morning.

I had the pleasure last Monday of meeting Auric at Darius Milhaud's, where I was lunching.

It was a great joy to find myself in the company of these two great artists for whom I have such a deep affection.

Yes, my dear Friend, these two artists are my consolation in the future and even in the present.

I'm mightily glad to know they are there, strong and bold.

I shall always march alongside these two men so full of steadfast courage.

Good day to the two Dadames, so good and kind to their old friend.

                    Amicalement votre
                              Erik Satie

While he got on very well with his young friends, Satie would have wished to include in the group some composers whose youthfulness — in his own words — lay above all 'in their character'. Thus he thought of drawing in Charles Koechlin, a remarkable teacher and an enlightened critic, fifty-one years old, who was distinguished physically by a long beard 'like a river god's'.

Erik Satie to Charles Koechlin
                    Arcueil-Cachan, 28 September 1918
Mon cher Ami — I have been instructed by the 'Nouveaux Jeunes' group to ask if you have any new — *or even old* — work that we could include in our programme of 19 Oct. — in the stately but congenial Salle Huyghens. We should like to have a quartet, a sonata for various instruments, etc. . . .

Do you have something?

Furthermore, the 'Nouveaux Jeunes' group requests me to address the following petition to you:

Become a member of our group, as above.

No subscription;

No rules;

No Committee;

Just — *Us*.

No presidency;

No treasury;

Nothing — but *Us*.

Come along with *Us*, as they say.

You agree? Yes?

You would give *Us* great pleasure, you know.

                    Bien à vous:
                              Erik Satie

Charles Koechlin to Erik Satie

Valmondois, Monday 30 September [1918]

Cher Ami, first of all thank you for your offer to welcome me into your group. I accept this offer willingly, seeing in it a mark of sympathy on the part of all of you, a mark of artistic sympathy that you certainly do not show to everyone (and you are quite right!); we are united by similar (if not the same) tastes, by sympathies and antipathies of the same kind; this is a good precondition for peace in our group. And then no committee, no president, no treasurer, these are all excellent innovations.

As to 19 October, I'm afraid I can't take part in your concert and I'm very sorry about that. The fact is I'm leaving shortly (for two months) for the United States along with other lecturers [. . .] But after my return to Paris I plan to put my first string quartet to work and then you might perhaps be able to fit it into one of these performances.

Croyez bien, cher Ami, à mes meilleures et bien dévouées amitiés

Charles Koechlin

By the time Koechlin got back from the United States, however, many things had changed. At the very moment when the Great War ended, Satie opened hostilities against the group which he himself had formed. One fine day Satie came to the house of Louis Durey, who was acting as the group's secretary, placed the following sealed letter in his hands and immediately left.

Erik Satie to Louis Durey

Friday 1 November 1918

Mon cher Durey,

Will you please be so kind as to consider me no longer a member of the 'Nouveaux Jeunes' group?

Amicalement vôtre

Erik Satie

Considering Satie to be an unpredictable person, Durey never questioned him as to the reasons for his resignation. Satie never spoke to him again. On the occasion of an evening organized by Pierre Bertin on behalf of the society 'Art et Liberté' founded by Edouard Autant and Louise Lara (later to become the well-known 'Art et Action'), Poulenc had the idea of arranging a kind of ceremony of reconciliation. Satie's reaction was quick in coming.

Erik Satie to Pierre Bertin

Thursday [November 1918]

Cher Ami — Poulenc's comico-idiotic manoeuvres — which everyone wants to make me 'swallow' and which utterly disgust me* — compel me to ask you to withdraw the 'homages' prepared for me by the good 'N.J.' gentlemen.

I won't accept them at any price. Let us look at other things: I have works by composers who remain much closer to me to submit to you.

Or else we could put together something quite different.

I shan't go to Valentine Gross's on Tuesday; and Cocteau has given me my liberty in respect of the *Séance Music Hall*. What luck! Ugh!

So I am free of all obligations in that direction.

That's why I want to have the same liberty at 'Art et Liberté', you see?

To play works by the 'N.J.' at my lecture, when I have *nothing* in common with them, would be to cause 'confusion'.

This we must not do.

Note, dear friend, that I'm not going to Valentine Gross's on Tuesday.

How're you doing? Did the Dadame get my little note? and the Demoiselle-Soeur?

Mille choses à tous trois de

ES

* As I'm perfectly entitled — it seems to me. I find it revolting when someone tries to make me like a fellow I can't stand.

P.S. Excuse this ugly paper: I'm writing to you in a 'caff'.

The truth is that Satie was not fond of collective undertakings, however restricted. But wishing to play the same role of animator and guide in relation to the new music that Apollinaire had fulfilled in respect of the new painting, Jean Cocteau undertook to gather together the scattered forces. Thus with Poulenc, Auric, Milhaud, Honegger, Durey and Tailleferre he created the Group of Six.

After agreeing to serve for a while as a 'fetish' for the Six who, at that moment, claimed his aesthetic as their own, Satie distanced himself as soon as he saw them comfortably installed in the artistic world of Paris. And he broke off all relations with those among them whom he judged guilty of arrivism.

Erik Satie to Charles Koechlin

Wednesday 6 February 1924

Cher Ami,

[. . .] I am very dissatisfied with the moral attitude of Poulenc and Auric and I find it necessary to separate myself from them. Lack of courage and character is one of the things that revolts me the most in the world.

And to think that these young men are wealthy! . . .

The faded laurels of Reynaldo Hahn make them squint with envy . . . It's sickening, I tell you. . .

But Milhaud remains magnificent.

Amicalement vôtre: ES

Another group of young men came along to place themselves under his patronage: Henri Sauguet, Maxime Jacob, Roger Désormière and Henri Cliquet-Pleyel. Since Satie had always said there would never be a 'School of Satie', these young men called themselves the 'Ecole d'Arcueil' [School of Arcueil], intending by this to express their aspiration for a music of essentials, a music that was as deliberately 'poor' as the little suburban district in which Satie had chosen to live.

After giving a talk on these new 'Nouveaux Jeunes' at the Collège de France — the same prestigious institution to which his father had taken him as a child — Satie presented their first concert at the Théâtre des Champs Elysées organized by Rolf de Maré.

Erik Satie to Rolf de Maré

Arcueil, 12 October 1923

Cher Directeur,

What is the 'Ecole d'Arcueil'? On 14 June I had the honour to introduce — at the Collège de France — four young musicians: Henri Cliquet-Pleyel, Roger Désormière, Maxime Jacob and Henri Sauguet.

They have given themselves the name 'Ecole d'Arcueil' out of friendship for an old inhabitant of this small suburb. Yes.

I shall not speak of their merits — being neither a schoolmaster nor a critic (fortunately).

The public is their only judge: it alone has the real power to express an opinion. . . Personally I am glad of this group's entry into the musical lists; it replaces the Six, who have naturally broken up and some of whom have become hopelessly famous — despite the absurd and comical statements of the '*artisses*', the '*perimés*' and the '*criticaillons*'.

Bien à vous: Erik Satie

Satie proved just as demanding, possessive and combative with the 'Ecole d'Arcueil' as he had always been. At this moment, Honegger and Roland Manuel had become his *bêtes noires*.

Erik Satie to Maxime Benjamin Jacob

Arcueil, 21 April 1923

Cher Monsieur,

See you Saturday 2 around 19 hours (7 o'clock). Chance brought the Mortier programme to my notice. I have nothing against Roland Manuel personally, but what an odd idea to put him with the 'Six'!

Do Auric and you want to be associated with him? That's your right, but it's also mine to find this mixture detestable. Why him and not Honegger? In any case — & I ask this in a friendly manner — do delete my name from this comical combination. I don't need to tell you that I'm dead set on this deletion: for me there can be no *union sacrée*, no dangerous compromises.

Bonjour, cher Monsieur. Till Saturday.

ES

Erik Satie to Henri Sauguet

Thursday 7 February 1924

Cher Ami — Thank you for your charming note [. . .]

Are you 'immovable'? If so, let's start a group with this title.

We must defend ourselves now or never. Yes.

Bien à vous

ES

Having acquired the habit, Satie saw no reason to stop. 'Now you no longer need me,' he said one day to his friends of the 'Ecole d'Arcueil'. 'I'm going to concern myself with younger people. . . ' He also said to Milhaud: 'I should so much like to know what kind of music the children who are now four years old will write.'

Satie loved young people, and the young returned his affection. It is among the youngest that we can see even today the greatest spontaneous interest in the music and personality of Erik Satie.

WARS

With the emergence of the Jeunes Ravêlites Satie had come out of his seclusion and resumed, or rather had begun, frequenting the salons. In particular, that of Cipa and Ida Godebski on the rue d'Athènes, which every Sunday evening brought together the musical avant-garde and a few literary outsiders, including Léon Paul Fargue. Cipa Godebski's sister Misia (who had been married first to Thadée Natanson, one of the owners of the *Revue Blanche*, then to Alfred Edwards, owner of the daily *Le Matin*, and who was now living with the Spanish painter José Maria Sert, whom she married after the war) was a key figure in Parisian society, whose fashions she created and destroyed for half a century. Gifted with unfailing taste and a definite charm, as well as a noteworthy capacity for intrigue, she treated the numerous geniuses she came across with great nonchalance. She has herself related, in her memoirs, how she crudely cut up with a pair of scissors certain canvasses by Bonnard that were too big for her walls, and one evening distributed to her guests to be used as paper hats dozens of letters from Proust, most of which she hadn't even bothered to open. Mallarmé, Vuillard, Toulouse-Lautrec were all in love with Misia. From the moment of his arrival in Paris Serge de Diaghilev, despite being a confirmed misogynist, never made an important decision without consulting her.

On 28 June 1914 Misia introduced Satie to Diaghilev. In her own words:

> Diaghilev was in Paris at that moment, and for some time I had been reproaching him with never having taken an interest in Erik Satie. In the end he gave in to my promptings and I brought them together at my home, so that Serge could hear the music of the Bon Maître d'Arcueil. Seated at the piano, the thin little Satie, pince-nez on his nose, had just finished playing his *Morceaux en forme de poire*, when an old friend of ours came rushing in, his beard bristling. In one breath he told us of the Sarajevo assassination and why war was logically inevitable. Leaning against the mantelpiece, my eyes shining with excitement, I listened fervently and I clearly remember that as he spoke I thought: "What luck! My God! Let there be war!. . ." My wish, as childish as it was unconsciously cruel, was not long in being fulfilled.

On 2 August general mobilization was ordered in France. Satie's young friends left for the front one after the other. There were now many of them to whom Satie might have written the same sort of letter he had sent to Roland Manuel a year earlier, when he left to do his military service.

Erik Satie to Roland Manuel

Arcueil, 26 October 1913

Mon pauvre vieux —

Is it going badly? Back pains? Or something else?

Do you love your officers? You must love them. I don't need to tell you that. Anyhow, you've got too much military spirit not to be a good soldier, a very good one.

Your officers are a constant example to you of discipline and war-like love. The longer you live with them the more vehemently you will love them.

Do you have the pleasure of seeing your flag, or some marvellous object of the same kind? What a beautiful thing a flag is! I must buy one.

I shall have it photographed and send you a print. Long live the Army, my friend!

Embrace your comrades for me, as I embrace you

ES

After the assassination of Jaurès on 31 July, Satie, on an impulse, had joined the Socialist Party. When France entered the war, he was immediately enrolled in the Socialist militia of Arcueil-Cachan.

Claude Debussy to the publisher Jacques Durand

Thursday 8 August 1914

Mon cher Jacques,

[. . .] You know that I have no sang-froid, and even less military spirit — never having had occasion to handle a gun — add to this memories of '70, which prevent me from giving way to enthusiasm, and the worries of my wife, whose son and son-in-law are in the army!

All this adds up to a life that is at once intense and troubled, in which I am nothing but a poor atom rolled hither and thither by this terrible cataclysm; what I am doing seems to me so terribly little! I even find myself envying Satie, who is seriously concerned with defending Paris in his role of corporal [. . .] Votre dévoué

Claude Debussy

Satie had attained the rank of corporal during a period of military training which he had been required to undertake — according to the practice of the time, which demanded that young men should regularly train for a few weeks each year — in spite of the setback he had experienced after volunteering in years gone by. On that occasion his brother received this message:

Erik Satie to Conrad Satie

23 February 1901

[. . .] At last I shall be in the bosom of a troop of men who are simple and bold, modest and heroic [. . .]

The Bilious Corporal

Enlisted-beard Corporal

Erik Satie

At the outbreak of the war, for a few days, or rather for a few nights, the Socialist militia of Arcueil led by Satie tirelessly scoured the streets 'armed to the teeth'. They were quickly asked to suspend their activities, because they were preventing people from sleeping.

Satie then returned to Montparnasse, which had meanwhile replaced Montmartre as the centre of artistic events in Paris. Instead of haunting the Chat Noir, the Auberge du Clou and the Lapin Agile cabarets, painters and poets now frequented the Dôme or the Rotonde cafés.

It was at the Rotonde that Edgard Varèse, just back from Berlin, where he had been working with Max Reinhardt on a spectacular production of *A Midsummer Night's Dream*, suggested mounting this same play in Paris to prove that Shakespeare was an 'ally' of the French and not of their enemies.

Satie had just dedicated one of his collections for piano, *Heures séculaires & instantanées*, 'to Sir William Grant-Plumot' [Great Penholder] whose 'continual immobility' he professed to admire. Varèse further confirmed the persistent success, through the centuries, of the man known at the Chat Noir as 'le grand Will'.

In these times of war most of the Paris theatres were closed, so the plan was to stage the *Dream* at the Cirque Médrano, an idea which almost automatically involved giving the roles of Bottom, Flute and Starveling to the Fratellini brothers, three famous clowns. In order not to owe anything to the 'Huns', Mendelssohn's music —

traditionally used for the *Dream* — was to be replaced by a
'pot-pourri' of French music specially composed by
Florent Schmitt, Stravinsky, Ravel, Varèse and Satie.
The latter, the only one to take this task seriously,
composed *Cinq Grimaces* for orchestra — a circus
orchestra, obviously.

Varèse later claimed to have contributed to the
orchestration of this score. It was just the kind of
assistance that Satie — who was often accused of 'not
knowing how to orchestrate' and had doubtless experienced some difficulties in this field — hardly appreciated.
Thus, when Varèse asked his permission to have this work
performed in the United States, it was almost certainly
from a need for revenge that Satie suggested replacing it
with a composition by one of his obscure pupils, which,
however, enjoyed the advantage of having been orchestrated by himself.

Erik Satie to Edgard Varèse

Arcueil, 6 February 1916

Bon Vieux Gros — Did you get my note of last Thursday? I
sent you *Gymnopédies* published by Rouart. I would ask you to
hold back on my music for *A Midsummer Night's Dream*.

Will you do that? Apart from that, the material isn't ready.

In exchange I'm sending you a strange piece by A. Verley
— one of my good pupils — a piece I have reduced to four
hands and orchestrated; or rather, I have orchestrated it and
reduced it to four hands. I recommend this piece. It is a real
collaboration. Read this work with your usual lucidity, mon
Gros Père. You will like its naive and tender simplicity.
Verley is a delicate colourist whom you can present to your
American friends. Let us back each other up, for heaven's
sake. I'm counting on you.

A bientôt

ES

The other day Debussy talked to me about you.

Pierre de Massot, who had an opportunity to see Varèse and Satie together at the beginning of the twenties, has given us his impression of their relations:

It wasn't Varèse's work Satie disliked, because I'm convinced he had never read a note of it, but the man himself. The old Norman fox, whose Scottish phlegm never left him under any circumstances, had no liking for the enthusiasm, petulance and Mediterranean volubility of the author of *Intégrales*. [. . .] One fine spring afternoon, Satie and I were drinking our *demies* of beer on the terrace of the Dôme. Suddenly Varèse appeared and, on seeing us, came over to our table. "Do you mind?" he asked. Satie grumbled between his teeth and Varèse, who hadn't heard, sat down [. . .] After a flood of polite remarks to the Bon Maître d'Arcueil, who remained silent, Varèse told us of the scandal caused in New York by the première of *Offrandes*, the rage of the audience, the intervention of the police. Then Satie, leaning over to me with one hand in front of his mouth in a familiar gesture, commented: "It's very simple, mon vieux, priests don't want to say Mass any more, concierges don't want to open the door. . ." And burst out laughing.

For his part, Varèse appreciated Satie and, even more, his work. He told Gunther Schuller: 'I've always admired Satie and above all the Kyrie of the *Messe des Pauvres*, which has always made me think of Dante's *Inferno* and strikes me as being a kind of pre-electronic music. . .'

For the staging of *A Midsummer Night's Dream* in Médrano, Varèse had commissioned the Cubist painter Albert Gleizes to design the costumes. A poet from the Right Bank, whom Gleizes had met in the home of his fiancée Juliette Roche, the daughter of an ambassador, suggested that he himself should make a French adaptation of the text. This poet was nicknamed 'le Prince frivole' after the title of one of his first works, but his real name was Jean Cocteau. He had already written the libretto of Reynaldo Hahn's *Le Dieu bleu* for the Ballets Russes. His translation of Shakespeare 'word for word with extensive cuts' was accepted.

Unfortunately the situation was not favourable to this kind of initiative. The plan to produce the *Dream* in Médrano was dropped all the more easily because Gleizes and Varèse had both finally decided to leave Paris for the United States. This brief adventure had, however, allowed Jean Cocteau to set foot on the Left Bank and even, as he was fond of saying himself, to place himself 'in the front line' of the art war. The state of war did not, in fact, prevent the artists, who for various reasons — age limit, foreign citizenship, war wounds — were still in Paris, from continuing to create their works and even bringing them to public attention.

Blaise Cendrars, who was already back from the front — the real one — minus one arm, along with the Pole Kisling, helped the Swiss painter Lejeune to fit out his disused studio in the rue Huyghens as a concert hall and art gallery.

On 18 April 1916 there was a 'Ravel-Satie' concert at the Salle Huyghens. Brought along by Misia, 'Tout Paris' was present for the occasion, including Jean Cocteau, who was on leave that day. Exempted from compulsory military service, Cocteau had volunteered for the Société Française de Secours aux Blessés, or Ambulance Corps, presided over by Count Etienne de Beaumont, and in the latter's company drove about in an ambulance car behind the Flanders front, dressed in a uniform cut by Paul Poiret.

This 18 April 1916 (not 1915, as he later mistakenly wrote) Cocteau had come to the Salle Huyghens accompanying his friend Valentine Gross, a young woman nicknamed the Swan because of her long neck, very gifted at drawing and with close ties — which was certainly not displeasing to the poet — to the eminent persons of the *Nouvelle Revue Française* who had the reputation of being difficult to get to know. The daughter of an Alsatian professor of music and a good musician herself, Valentine numbered among her friends several composers, among them Edgard Varèse, Roland Manuel and Erik Satie.

The 'Ravel-Satie' concert was introduced by Roland Manuel, who stressed the originality of the work and personality of Erik Satie. Published at the author's expense, Roland Manuel's introduction served as a basis for the view of Satie later propagated by Cocteau.

Erik Satie to Roland Manuel

Wednesday 19 April 1916

Petit Gros Vieux — you were such a brick yesterday that I simply must thank you.

I listened attentively to your talk. It was perfect. You have done a lot for me already: yesterday you added the final touch.

Je vous embrasse de tout coeur: ES

Ricardo Viñes, who was at the piano that day, had played *Morceaux en forme de poire* as a four-handed piece with the composer.

Erik Satie to Ricardo Viñes

Wednesday 19 April 1916

Vieux et Cher Complice —

I embrace you with all my heart.

I shall never be able to thank you enough.

How *emmerdante* my old music is!

What *connerie*, I venture to say!

Votre vieux camarade et ami: ES

After listening to *Morceaux en forme de poire* (which Satie was certainly the only one to find '*emmerdante*' [very boring]), Valentine Gross no doubt told Cocteau that during one evening reception Roland Manuel, to entertain his friends, had amused himself by choreographing this score in the style of *Schéhérazade*, the most famous of the pre-war Ballets Russes shows.

Seizing upon this idea, Cocteau thought of repeating this drawing-room game in earnest. After the semi-failure of *Le Dieu bleu*, he was desperately looking for an idea capable of 'astonishing' Diaghilev, as the latter had expressly demanded. These 'pieces in the shape of a pear', looked to him like the dreamed-of opportunity. So the very next day he asked Valentine to put him in touch with Satie. What he had not foreseen was Satie's reaction.

La Poire d'Erik Satie

Erik Satie to Valentine Gross

25 April 1916

Chère Amie,

I have flu like a horse.

Getting better. Tomorrow at your place. See you.

I hope the admirable Cocteau won't use any of my old works.

Let's do something new, right?

Pas de blague.   Votre vieux camarade: ES

Satie was certainly not opposed to collaborating with Cocteau. Every fresh opportunity to compose a new work was welcome to him. What he did not want was 'to do something new with something old'. So he set about pointing Cocteau in the right direction.

Erik Satie to Jean Cocteau

Tuesday [25 April 1916]

Cher Ami — Excuse me. Sick: with the flu.

Impossible to warn you except by telepathy.

Tomorrow, agreed.

Valentine Gross tells me wonderful things. You are the man with Ideas. Bravo!

Votre vieux: ES

Two years earlier, with Stravinsky in mind, Cocteau had conceived the idea of a ballet inspired by the biblical legend of King David. The better to captivate the composer of *Petrushka*, Cocteau had visualized the various episodes as being performed on a fairground stage. In spite of these efforts, Stravinsky had shown no interest.

Meanwhile the project — also to come to nothing — of a performance of *A Midsummer Night's Dream* at Médrano had helped to fix the poet's eye on fairground spectacles. Compelled by Satie to think up 'new' ideas, he imagined three numbers presented by barkers: a Chinese conjuror, an American dancer and an Acrobat. 'The Chinese was capable of torturing missionaries, the Little Girl of going down with the Titanic, the Acrobat of being on confidential terms with the Stars'. Pursuing this last image, Massine, the choreographer of *Parade*, devised for the Acrobat a pas de deux to be danced in the company of a Star. Picasso improvised the costume of this additional character by painting stars directly onto the dancer's tights. History finally retained from this number only the dance of 'a pair of Acrobats'.

In the first set of notes, the 'Little Girl' (who was to go down with the Titanic) was called more precisely 'A Young American Girl'. In this connection it is not without interest to know that No 22 of the *Soirées de Paris* (Apollinaire's review to which Cocteau was a subscriber) was illustrated, among other things, by reproductions of two pictures by Picabia, entitled respectively *Udnie, a young American girl (dance)* and *Prima Ballerina on a Transatlantic Liner*.

Cocteau found the title for his ballet *Parade* in the Larousse, from which he copied out this definition: 'a burlesque scene played at the door of a fairground theatre to attract customers'. Before leaving for Flanders, he sent all his notes in bulk to Satie. The same day he posed for Picasso to whom he had been introduced by Varèse.

Jean Cocteau to Valentine Gross

1 May [1916]

Ma chère Valentine [. . .] This morning I posed for Picasso.
He is starting a very 'Ingres' head of me to serve as a
frontispiece for a young Poet's works after his premature
death [. . .] Thanks to you I've sent a big bundle of work to
Arcueil [. . .]

Je vous baise les mains

Vôtre Jean

Erik Satie to Jean Cocteau

2 May [1916]

Cher Ami — I received the manuscript. Stunning! I'm
sorting out my ideas. You'll write to me, won't you?

There's enough work here for a horse.

I'm in the process of sizing it all up.

A vous de tout coeur

ES

Jean Cocteau to Valentine Gross

[3 May 1916]

[. . .] Express letter from Satie. 'Stunning', he says. Does
that indicate enthusiasm in his Faun's language? Try to find
out [. . .]

Jean

On 6 May Cocteau returned to his ambulance service, but
his heart was no longer in it.

Jean Cocteau to Valentine Gross

[May 1916]

[. . .] From one day to the next I've lost my balance. I
suppose *Parade* is a dream, it's impossible to imagine I am
anything but this frozen wreck travelling the roads. I
swallow my tears [. . .]

12 May 1916

Ma chère Valentine

Strange exhaustion [. . .] Worried *Parade* — worried 'source' — 'zest' etc. Worried your work [. . .] Sad.

Jean

For the moment, Cocteau's anguish was unjustified, because Satie was not merely still keen on the realization of their joint project but was busy putting it on a firm foundation. He calculated rightly that, to make sure of Diaghilev's agreement, they must first gain the approval of Misia. It was to Misia that he dedicated the version of *Parade* for piano duet.

Erik Satie to Misia Edwards

Arcueil-Cachan, 15 May 1916

Chère Madame,

Matisse, Picasso and other *Bons Messieurs* are giving a 'Granados-Satie' concert on 30 May at Bongard's.

Since your presence at rue Huyghens brought me luck (yes, Madame), I would ask you to act as my patron at this new ceremony. Will you?

What you told me about the Ballets Russes has already produced an effect: I'm working on something which I plan to show you very shortly and which is dedicated to you in thinking of it and in writing it.

All this, chère Madame, gives me the greatest pleasure.

I have learned that at this moment you are creating a 'bird-tree'. You must be a magician.

Respectueusement vôtre: ES

The 'bird-tree' created by Misia was an ornamental tree composed of plumage and pearls. Misia's niece, Mimi Godebska, aged fifteen, had just written a short poem in prose, *Daphénéo*, to a melody by Satie, in which we learn that 'bird-trees' are trees that produce, instead of fruit, 'weeping birds': an allusion, no doubt, to those birds that weep when their plumage is torn out, and also a wink to

Ravel (a great friend of Mimi's to whom he had dedicated *Ma Mére l'Oye*), who also wrote *Oiseaux tristes*.

Satie liked to work in an atmosphere of calm, with time to mature his plans. 'Before writing a work,' he said, 'I walk around it several times and I get myself to go with me'. When Cocteau, still anxious, started harassing him from a distance, Satie put things straight once and for all.

Erik Satie to Jean Cocteau

Thursday morning, 8 June 1916

Cher Ami — Don't worry, don't be nervous: I'm working. Let me get on with it, *bon vieux*.

Be informed that I shan't show you the work until October. You won't see a note before then. I swear to that!

Will you give me permission to say that you are the author of the theme? I need that. Madame Edwards is supporting this work. I've told her she will have to wait until October. I want to do something good, very good: you must trust me.

If you come to Paris, let me know.

Amitiés to Valentine Gross & yourself

ES

This letter, which was supposed to be reassuring, in fact plunged Cocteau into despair. That Misia might learn that he was working on a project for Diaghilev without first consulting her, was enough in itself to turn her against him. Moreover, she did not, as a rule, lend her support to any works not inspired, in one way or another, by herself, and would never have tolerated seeing herself supplanted by Valentine in her chosen role of intermediary. And Diaghilev never listened to anyone but her! Cocteau made an extreme effort to cover his tracks and recover lost ground with two successive notes.

Satie
1916

Jean 1916

Jean Cocteau to Misia Edwards

[June 1916]

Chère Misia,

A letter from Erik Satie has cancelled my promise of silence. One evening at your house, during a moving encounter, Satie asked for my collaboration just as I was about to ask for his. This little intimate miracle took place in front of Valentine Gross, who was thereby informed of it. I have kept the secret until I was sure that the work was 'in full swing', having suffered too much from haste with Stravinsky. There was also Satie's formal wish. No doubt too, although there is nothing left of *David*, *David* came to nothing in order to give birth to the new thing — mysteries surpass men. You will be the first to understand, therefore it is to you that I now make the announcement — abandoning the incognito (for you alone) as soon as Satie asked me to. We shall only accept your 'love' — a simple 'approval' would kill the poor minstrels from Arcueil-Anjou. It is a very short work that is just like the musician. Everything takes place behind a pince-nez [. . .]

[June–July 1916]

Chère Misia [. . .] Satie is an angel (well disguised). . . May our collaboration move you as it moved me the day I told him what he was to write [. . .] I deduce from his notes that things are moving along in the direction I most wish for. It is *his* drama and the eternal drama played out between the audience and the stage. . . You know my love, my worship for Igor. . . Above all, never let him imagine that I am 'grafting' a slip from *David*. . . I ran into Igor while walking without knowing it towards Satie and perhaps Satie is at the corner of a street that will bring me back to Igor.

In short, the Stravinsky-Cocteau adventure was *heavy* and full of misunderstandings.

Our meeting with Satie represents only light happiness [. . .]

Jean

Nevertheless, this happiness risked being seriously compromised. On the one hand, Misia had realized that Cocteau was trying to pull the wool over her eyes and secretly prepared her revenge; on the other, Satie himself had suggested another subject for a ballet to Diaghilev: an adaptation of La Fontaine's *Fables* by the young poet René Chalupt, in a setting by Charles Stern. A wealthy man with private means, a patron of the arts, something of a Maecenas, Stern was at this time engaged to Valentine Gross. 'He himself,' according to Jean Hugo, 'did very black and white drawings in the style of the Munich exhibition of 1910, a bit like Georges Lepape or Charles Martin.'

At this particular moment Satie was no doubt looking with greater favour upon Chalupt's project than upon Cocteau's. On the one hand, the relaxed attitude of the former suited him better than the harassment of the latter; on the other, he did not like in principle — as we shall also see on the occasion of *Relâche* — to collaborate with someone who was physically distant. As for Misia, she brought all her energy to bear in favour of the La Fontaine project, in the secret hope of causing Cocteau's to be forgotten and thus meting out to the latter the punishment he deserved. Her tendency to cause the abortion of projects which she did not entirely control, soon gained her the nickname the *Faiseuse d'Anges* (abortionist).

Erik Satie to Misia Edwards

Arcueil-Cachan, 9 July 1916

Chère Dame — I'm coming on Tuesday, aren't I? If that's right, not a word: I shall arrive myself. I've thought a lot about my little idea of doing the *Fables*. That will work out, & I want you to like it.

The Cocteau 'thing' will come later. I am in no way abandoning it. I'm not a quitter. And I don't imagine Diaghilev is a man to go back on his acceptance, is he?

These *Fables* will enable us to be very modern, because, without turning a hair, we reject *pastiche*. A fig for that!

Bon vieux La Fontaine will go purple in the face, le pauvre. As a matter of fact, a friend of mine lives in his street, in Passy. I shall go and walk around the district: that will inspire me.

I'm going to your brother's this evening. Will you be there?

Bonjour, Chère Dame.

Respectueusement vôtre: ES

However, things were to work out differently. In the end it was *Parade* that was performed. When the time came to publish her memoirs, Misia did not hesitate to rearrange history a little, touching up her facts where necessary. This is the version of the foregoing letter from Satie which she presented in 1950:

Erik Satie to Misia Edwards

Chère Dame — I'm coming on Tuesday, aren't I? If that's right, not a word to the others about what I have prepared for you. My little idea for the 'thing' has matured so well that I shall be able to play it to you right to the end (there's a little verse missing around the middle, but I count on you not to say so). And I want you to like it.

A lot of evil people are saying I've abandoned it for my *Fables*. I'm not a quitter. And I don't imagine Diaghilev is a man to go back on his acceptance, is he?

The *bon* La Fontaine will wait. We shall only be very modern and shall without turning a hair reject *pastiche*. A fig for that! Our *bon vieux* will go purple in the face. . . But first let's win the victory of the 'thing'.

Bonjour, chère Dame.

E.S.

And Misia commented that the 'thing' — that is to say *Parade* — did indeed win a true victory, even adding that she had been overjoyed by the fact that Cocteau had shared in this success.

However, events did not pan out as joyfully as she would have us believe. The letters that Valentine Gross was receiving regularly at this period enable us to follow the development of the situation step by step.

Erik Satie to Valentine Gross

13 July 1916

Chère Amie,

Permit me to wish you a happy Quatorze Juillet. That's the least of things. So don't thank me.

How are you?

As far as I'm concerned, I'm not working: I'm overcome by a terrible depression I can't shake off. That's bad.

I feel like playing dirty tricks on the poor world.

As a matter of fact, I am playing them. . .

You, chère Amie, are sheltered from these 'reprisals'.

I've seen Diaghilev and reached an agreement with him. I submitted an idea which he liked, all the more because he was looking for something along these lines and couldn't find anything. I shall have a series of things here that are 'my own'. You understand?

We make a nice pair. Will he diddle me? Probably.*

So much the worse for him.

Chère Amie, bonjour. Come back soon

ES

* I'm not beginning this 'thing' without an advance. Am I wrong? No.

As Satie gave him no further sign of life, Cocteau managed to get another leave at the end of July and went to Paris, which he never again left. For several days, in the spirit of the 'dirty tricks' we have heard about, Satie did not reply to his pressing calls.

Jean Cocteau to Valentine Gross

[Paris, 13 July 1916]

[. . .] I have a feeling of anguish and crazy loneliness. . . I beg you to give a sign, exorcise the devil, see Satie and find out. I'm dying of disappointment [. . .]

5 August 1916

Ma chère Valentine,

I'm atrociously sad, confused. What can I do? Contact with you is my only comfort. Im-pos-si-ble to work. Help!

Jean

It was at this moment that something went wrong between Misia and Satie. After having manoeuvred to separate the composer from Cocteau, she no doubt dreamed of causing the La Fontaine project to founder likewise. It seems that she announced in front of a sufficient number of people to be sure it would get to the ears of the person concerned: 'Satie is old. Let him stay old, that's fine. . .'

For a long time Satie never again referred to her except under the names *Aunt Trufaldin* or *Aunt Brutus*. José-Maria Sert, who lived with her, henceforth became *Uncle Brutus*.

Erik Satie to Valentine Gross

Tuesday 3.12 p.m. [8 August 1916]

That's it! I've had a row with Aunt Trufaldin. What a cow! Yes.

I'm going to see Cocteau tomorrow morning.

Bonjour, chère Amie. You're a good sort, good and straight.

Succeed with such skunks? No [. . .]   ES

As always, it was Cocteau who straightened things out.

Jean Cocteau to Valentine Gross

9 August 1916

[. . .] A very good day with Satie. . . The Erik-Trufaldin disaster not serious and very serious [. . .]

12 August 1916

[. . .] The good Satie (Arcueil) is composing wonders for me and refuses to see Aunt Brutus [. . .]

Jean

Erik Satie to Valentine Gross

Thursday [10 August 1916]

That's right, chère amie, Cocteau is stunning.

We're working solidly and with joy. The Aunt will be less visible. It's better that way: she doesn't amuse me. Uncle ditto.

You're a wonderful friend. Yes. Come back quickly.

Vôtre vieux: ES

This note is calligraphed on the back of a postcard showing a picture by Tade Styka of a young man on horseback. Underneath it Satie has written: 'Me and my horse from *Parade*'. So a horse had already been introduced into the round dance performed by the Chinese, the American Girl and the Acrobat. Other essential figures were not long in making their appearance in the story.

Jean Cocteau and Erik Satie to Valentine Gross

24 August 1916

Picasso is doing *Parade* with us.

Jean   Erik

All his life, Cocteau flattered himself with the thought that he had drawn Picasso into designing for the stage:

In Montparnasse, in 1916, the grass was still growing between the paving stones. Greengrocers were pushing street. It was between the Rotonde and the Dôme that I asked Picasso to do *Parade* [. . .] His friends didn't believe he would take up my suggestion. There was a dictatorship weighing upon Montmartre and Montparnasse. We were going through the austere period of Cubism. The objects you might find on a café table, a Spanish guitar, were the only pleasures permitted. To paint a stage set, especially for the Ballets Russes (these young people knew nothing of Stravinsky), was a crime.

The experience of the theatre was to be very fruitful for the painter for whom it provided an opportunity to study forms and colours in three-dimensional space. That he should participate in *Parade* was no doubt fated. Had he not been painting a portrait of Cocteau the very day Cocteau sent his first notes to Satie?

With Picasso, Cocteau now held a trump card. Nevertheless, his calvary was not yet quite at an end.

Jean Cocteau to Valentine Gross

31 August 1916

[. . .] Picasso and Satie get on like Misia and Serge [. . .]

4 September 1916

[. . .] Make dear Satie understand, through the haze of apéritifs, that I do after all have some part in *Parade* and that he's not alone with Picasso. I believe *Parade* to be a kind of renewal of the theatre and not a mere 'opportunity' for music. He hurts my feelings when he jumps up and down and shouts to Picasso: 'It's you I follow! You're my master!' He seems to be hearing for the first time things I've been telling him over and over again. Does he hear my voice? Perhaps this is merely an acoustical phenomenon. Anyhow, I'm probably exaggerating the way sick people do [. . .] The Swan would quickly make Satie understand lots of puzzles and calm his excessive hatred of the Aunt. Ssh — not a word

— because the work is going forward and that's the main thing. Picasso is thinking up wonders and Satie's American Girl is almost finished [. . .] The little American girl in *Parade* makes her entry like this: on the 47th floor an angel has made her nest in the dentist's office — and there's this little song: 'Tic tic tic Titanic toc toc the Titanic is plunging lights ablaze into the sea' [. . .]

Jean

Erik Satie to Valentine Gross

Thursday, 14 September 1916

Chère et douce Amie — Very sweet, your letter. Thank you. If only you knew how sad I am! *Parade* is changing, for the better, behind Cocteau's back! Picasso has ideas I like better than our Jean's!

What a calamity! And I'm for Picasso! and Cocteau doesn't know it! What can I do?

Picasso told me to continue working on Jean's text and he, Picasso, will work on another text, his own — which is breathtaking! Fabulous!

I'm growing crazy and sad! What can I do! Knowing Picasso's fine ideas, I'm heartbroken to be forced to compose to those of the good Jean, less fine — oh yes! less fine!

What to do? What to do? — Write and advise me. I'm going crazy. All the best to Stern.

Tout plein bonjour à vous:

ES

The differences between the poet and the painter related to new characters which Picasso had imagined — three imposing Managers — and also to the dialogue, consisting essentially of onomatopoeias, which Cocteau insisted on retaining against the advice of his team-mates. Nevertheless, everything worked out for the best.

Erik Satie to Valentine Gross

Wednesday [20 September 1916]

Chère Amie — It's all fixed. Cocteau knows everything. He

and Picasso have come to an understanding. What luck!

How're you? Are you working?

I am. I wish you could hear.

See you soon, eh?

Votre vieil ami: ES

P.S. Did I tell you I'm making a nice pair with Diaghilev? Still no money from him. The Aunt is in Rhum — I mean Rome.

Jean Cocteau to Valentine Gross

[22 September 1916]

[. . .] You were probably worried about Satie. Let me reassure you at once. Our good Socrates is creating confusion between Picasso and me — and imagines one is saying white and the other black because of differences of vocabulary. We've decided with Picasso to lie so that he goes along without getting everything confused [. . .]

Jean

In fact, it was Cocteau who had given way all along the line, as is clearly shown by the final shape of the ballet. The Managers and their gloomy stamping dominated the stage. No dialogue was left.

On 7 October 1916 everyone, now reconciled, met at the house of a wealthy Chilean woman, Madame Eugenia Errazuriz. Serge de Diaghilev brought with him a young dancer, Léonide Massine, to whom he entrusted the choreography of *Parade*. Only Misia, on holiday in Rome, was missing. Cocteau did not fail to bring her up to date.

Jean Cocteau to Misia Edwards

[10 October 1916]

Chère Misia,

Come back quickly. I'm in a hurry to throw my arms round your neck and forget in a good laugh and good embraces a thousand mix-ups caused by distance and exhaustion. A very good meeting with Serge and Massine, whose fresh intelligence and bearing appeal to me greatly. It seems to me that Serge likes our work and that he has very well understood the apparently simple way in which I have brought about the marriage of the musician and the painter. I gave them a hand in the middle. . .

No doubt he will tell you about the Babel evening when Madame Errazuriz shouted in Spanish with Picasso, Serge in Russian with Massine and Satie in Sauternes with me [. . .]

Jean

In the midst of storms, interspersed with breaks in the clouds, Satie continued to work slowly but surely. 'Little by little,' said Cocteau, 'there came into being a sober, clear score, in which the composer seemed to have discovered an unknown dimension thanks to which we attend, simultaneously, the outer and the inner show.'

Erik Satie to Valentine Gross

1 September 1916

[. . .] The Chinese is finished. He doesn't have a bad 'trumpet'. I would have liked to play it for you. I'm after the 'American dancer'. That's going pretty well, you'll see [. . .]

ES

Erik Satie to Jean Cocteau

Thursday 19 Oct. 1916

Cher Ami — Thank you for your note.

I've been working on our 'thing', very hard.

The 'little American girl' is doing fine.

The 'rag' is in good health; it fits in well. However, I won't be able to show it to you tomorrow, because I can't work on it this afternoon. You'll be 'dumbfounded' at the audition.

The 'wave movement' will be very effective after the 'rag'. Placed thus, it will do well, very well.

I've written a lot for our 'thing'. A lot.

Believe me, Cher Ami.
Till tomorrow.
My regards to Madame Cocteau.

Vôtre vieux: ES

Erik Satie to Valentine Gross

[2 December 1916]

[. . .] I have written the *Petit prélude du Rideau rouge*. It's an introduction to the fugue, very *meditative*, very *serious*, and even somewhat 'boring', but short. I like this kind of thing, slightly conventional and falsely naive, completely 'kono', as the 'Japons' say [. . .]

ES

Picasso had made use of the curtain to show 'the reverse of the scenery': a poetic fairy vision of fairground life, recalling his 'blue period' and contrasting with the 'heaviness' of the Managers. Concerning the *Prélude du Rideau rouge* [Prelude on the Red Curtain], Roland Manuel noted that the composer 'has pushed deference to the painter to the point of composing a piece of music for no other reason than to salute him.' In origin, the score of this piece bore the sub-title: 'Homage to Picasso'.

Erik Satie to Valentine Gross

[2 January 1917]

Chère Amie — Viñes and I will be rehearsing tomorrow at 4bis, rue du Sergent Hoff, at 2 o'clock. Are you coming?
    I've finished *Parade*. At last![. . .]

ES

In the meantime Picasso was working like a dog, while Massine was showing impatience to get involved as well.

Léonide Massine to Jean Cocteau

27 January [1917]

Mon cher Cocteau,

I've just written a few words to Picasso expressing my keenness to work with him. Not only with him, of course, but also with our dear Satie and with you. M. Diaghilev is enchanted with the music and the general conception of the work [. . .] You can be sure I shall do my best [. . .]

Léonide Massine

Pablo Picasso to Jean Cocteau

Montrouge, 1 February 1917

Mon cher Jean,

Massine will be pleased. You can write to him. Everything will work out. I'm working on our matter almost every day. No one should worry [. . .]

Pablo

Soon after this, the Ballets Russes left for Rome, where they were to put on a performance at the Teatro Costanzi. Diaghilev asked the authors of *Parade* to follow him to 'marry set, music and choreography'.

Jean Cocteau to Valentine Gross

11 February 1917

[. . .] Diaghilev is carrying us off in his cyclone — Picasso, Satie and me — the huge pink rhinoceros is taking us on his horn all the way to Rome. Satie is buying 'bags' [. . .]

16 February 1917

[. . .] We're off tomorrow without Satie. Impossible to take this strange parcel with pawpaws along with us. When the Minister asked him 'Do you know Rome, Monsieur Satie?' he replied: 'By name . . . only by name!' [. . .]

Jean

In fact Satie preferred to stay in Arcueil. 'He doesn't like moving his fine musical wine', said Cocteau. Cocteau and Picasso went to Rome. 'It's our honeymoon', they joked to Gertrude Stein. A presentiment? It was in Rome that Picasso met Olga Koklova, his future wife.

The Montparnasse painters grimaced. 'The Cubist code', explains Cocteau, 'forbade any travel except that from north to south in Paris between the Place des Abbesses and the Boulevard Raspail [. . .] Picasso laughed to see the figures of his painter friends shrink as the train moved away'.

In Rome the Managers assumed their final shape as character-decor ('for the first time a set took part in the play instead of merely being present'), largely thanks to the participation of the Futurist Fortunato Depero, already the creator of Constructivist personages of painted cardboard. Even as he decried the Italian Futurists in his letters to Misia, calling them 'provincial and boastful', Cocteau based himself on their aesthetic theories in demanding the presence of mechanical noises in the score.

Far from opposing him, Satie had no hesitation in asserting later that all he had done was to compose 'a fund of certain sounds which the librettist considered indispensable to create the atmosphere for his characters'. Georges Auric, his mouthpiece at this period, wrote that 'the music of *Parade* submits humbly to present-day reality, which stifles the song of the nightingale beneath the rumble of tramcars'.

The man responsible for this symbolic stifling was not in the least bothered by this unflattering description. Considering these noises a legitimate compensation for the dialogues he had been persuaded to suppress, he boasted, on the contrary, of being 'the first poet not to express himself in words'. He forgot the Futurist sound poems and the 'Poème bruitiste' (noisist poem) by Huelsenbeck introduced by Tzara in Zurich in 1916. However, it was no doubt because Tzara had compared

M. L

'the use of noises in poetry to the objective reality the Cubists set down on their canvasses' that Cocteau described *Parade* as a 'realist' ballet.

Approving the choice of this adjective, Apollinaire, who had been entrusted with writing an introduction for the programme at the Châtelet, felt the need to reinforce it. This was how he came to invent the word *sur-réalisme*, which enjoyed the success we know.

Cocteau visibly suffered seeing that the press, ignoring his claim, instead of blaming him, poked fun at Satie. The latter was not too pleased either at seeing himself accused of being 'a composer of music for typewriters'. At every performance the poet was further tormented by the imperfect manner in which these sounds were reproduced. At the same time, the role that he himself had played in the creation of this work acquired even greater importance in his eyes.

It was Valentine Gross (meanwhile married to Jean Hugo) who received Satie's confidence on this subject.

Erik Satie to Valentine Hugo

13 December 1920

[. . .] *Parade* will be done on the 21st of this month. Cocteau continues his 'boring' tricks of 1917. He's 'boring' Picasso and me till I'm shattered.

It's a mania with him: *Parade* is his work alone. That's fine with me. But why didn't he make the scenery and the costumes and why didn't he compose the music for this poor ballet?

ES

After the 1920 revival, André Gide noted in his journal:

Went to see *Parade* at the Théâtre des Champs Elysées. Cocteau was strolling backstage where I went to see him; he looked aged, drawn, in pain. He's well aware that Picasso created the scenery and costumes and

Satie the music, but he is wondering whether Picasso and Satie have been created by himself.

On the occasion of another production of *Parade*, at the Théâtre de la Gaîté on 19 June 1923, Satie wrote to Diaghilev: 'I don't much like the "noises" made by Jean. There's nothing to be done about that: we have before us a charming maniac'.

The première of the ballet, on 18 May 1917 at the Châtelet, had been particularly stormy. Cocteau went so far as to say that 'it was the greatest battle of the war', and then, pushing the metaphor, he added: 'I've heard the shouts that accompany a bayonet charge in Flanders, but that was nothing compared to what happened that night at the Théâtre du Châtelet'. In fact, it did not happen at night but one afternoon. Some people, in any case, saw in the din made that day on the stage and in the auditorium, a foretaste of the explosion of the shells soon to be fired at Paris.

Erik Satie to Roland Manuel

14 March 1918

Mon vieux — there very nearly wasn't any more Satie: I very nearly got killed. The shells were terribly close to me! I thought I was done for! People were killed, but not me. A bit of luck, eh! Although only a civilian, I stood the test [. . .]

Erik Satie

By chance, Blaise Cendrars witnessed this event. Later he described it to the journalist Michel Manoll:

One night of shelling, in 1918, one of the last and most violent of the war, I saw a man lying at the foot of the Obelisk, Place de la Concorde. I bent over him, thinking he was dead. It was my old friend Satie. 'What are you doing there?' I asked him. He replied: 'I know it's ridiculous and that I'm not in the shelter. But what the hell, that thing there sticks up into the air and I have the feeling of being sheltered. So I'm composing a piece of music for the Obelisk. Isn't that nice, eh?' — 'Yes', I told him, 'so long as it isn't a military march'. — 'Oh, right', he said. 'There's no danger. It's music for the Pharaonne who is buried underneath it. No one ever thinks of her. It took these stinking shells to make me. It's the first time. Say, this thing's not bad, is it. . .' And he laughed, his hand on his beard as usual, his malicious eyes scanning the monument. 'Do you know who is buried under it?' I asked Satie. 'It seems it's the mummy of Cleopatra. At least, that's what I've been told.' — 'You don't say,' replied Satie. 'Then I was right to make a little music for her. Listen:

Ta, tarâ, ta, ta, ta, ta, ta
ta, tarâ, ta, ta, ta, ta. . .
Fa, do-ô, sol, re, la, mi, si — Fa, do-ô, sol, re, la, mi.'

LAWSUITS

Among the Parisian music critics — his 'faithful enemies' — Satie singled out Jean Poueigh for a bitter and far-reaching quarrel.

Satie had first noticed Poueigh in 1911 on the publication of a book, *Musiciens français d'aujourd'hui*, which he had written under the pseudonym Octave Séré in order to be able to celebrate his own work as a composer, which he signed with his true name. In a chapter devoted to Debussy, Séré-Poueigh had briefly mentioned — not without stating that 'not too much importance should be attached to it' — the name of Erik Satie, 'a clumsy but subtle technician engaged in the search for delightful, often bizarre new sonorities. *Deuxième Sarabande*, written in 1887, left a deep impression on M. Debussy'.

Satie first replied by publishing in the *Revue musicale S.I.M.* a 'fragment' from his *Mémoires d'un Amnésique: 'Ce que je suis'*. In an exercise in 'ironical conformism', at which he had become a master, he adopted an attitude completely in keeping with Poueigh's, assuring the reader that he did, indeed, derive more pleasure from measuring a sound than from hearing it: 'phonometer in hand I work joyfully and confidently'. For some time he continued to present himself as a 'phonometrographer'. Thus, he one day wrote the following letter to the great pianist Ricardo Viñes, whom he wished to be the interpreter of his own works.

Erik Satie to Ricardo Viñes

30 March 1912

Monsieur, I came to see you yesterday with my friend
Roland Manuel to ask you to permit me to dedicate one of
my *Pièces froides* to you.

I should be happy if you would accept this frail homage
rendered to an artist who has done so much for modern
music.

Don't imagine that my work is music. That's not my line. I
do, to the best of my ability, phonometry. Nothing else. Am I
anything else than an acoustician without great knowledge?

Have you received my *Sarabandes*, my *Morceaux en forme de
poire* and my *Habit de Cheval*? I asked Lerolle to send them to
you. Tell me, please, if that has been done.

Recevez, Monsieur, mes sentiments admiratifs et cor-
diaux

Erik Satie

The second and final encounter between Satie and
Poueigh took place on the occasion of *Parade*. Staged by
the Ballets Russes at the Châtelet, on 18 May 1917, at the

height of the war, this ballet by Satie, Picasso and Cocteau was seen by the public as a bomb in the true sense of an engine of destruction for the benefit of the enemy. Its very novelty was considered an act of aggression against the traditional patriotic values which the soldiers at the front were in the process of defending at the risk of their lives. There was no lack of jealous and envious people to reinforce this interpretation by pointing out that several of those responsible were already very much compromised. Diaghilev had just celebrated the deposition of the Czar by hoisting the red flag on the stage of the theatre, and Picasso was known as one of 'Kahnweiler's cubists', having been under contract to this German art dealer whom hostilities had compelled to seek refuge in Switzerland.

In *Les Carnets de la Semaine* Jean Poueigh had deplored this 'ballet that outrages French taste' no more and no less violently than his colleagues, but what particularly exasperated Satie was the fact that Poueigh had attacked him after congratulating him at the end of the performance. Satie immediately sent him a series of postcards.

Erik Satie to Jean Poueigh

30 May 1917

[. . .] What I know is you are an ass-hole — and, if I dare say so — an unmusical 'ass-hole'. Above all, never again offer me your dirty hand [. . .]

Erik Satie

Erik Satie to Monsieur Jean Poueigh
Head Flop
Chief Gourds and Turkey

3 June 1917

[. . .] You're not as dumb as I thought [. . .] Despite your bonehead air and your short-sightedness, you see things at a great distance [. . .]

Erik Satie

Erik Satie to Monsieur Fuckface Poueigh
Famous Gourd and Composer for Nitwits
                    Fontainebleau, 5 June 1917
[. . .] Lousy ass-hole, this is from where I shit on you with all
my force [. . .]
                              Erik Satie

We have only these few extracts as they were transcribed
in the Court verdict for the suit for slander that Poueigh
hastened to institute against Satie on the grounds that
these open postcards had no doubt been read by his own
concierge.

In view of this lawsuit, Apollinaire, who had defended
Parade with the authority of a well-known poet and a war
veteran, insisted on introducing Satie to Maître José
Théry. Five years before, this lawyer had proved himself
very efficient when Apollinaire had been suspected of
having stolen some Iberian sculptures, and perhaps even
the Mona Lisa, from the Louvre.

Guillaume Apollinaire to Maître José Théry
                              24 June [1917]

Mon cher ami,

I am sending you Erik Satie, against whom, following
Parade, Jean Poueigh has started a suit for slander. The first
slanderer was Mr Poueigh, who has no feeling for modern
art, always confusing it — oddly — with 'Hunnish' art.

In short, if Erik Satie comes to you, I have no doubt you
will get him out of the mess he has got himself into by telling
M. Poueigh the truth.
              In friendship
                    Guill. Apollinaire

This move did not prove fortunate, for Maître Théry had
already been chosen as his defence counsel by Poueigh.
For a long time Satie remained convinced that Apollinaire
had intended to make fun of him. He faced the Court on 12
July flanked by the less distinguished Maître Peytel.

Erik Satie to Ricardo Viñes

[July 1917]

[. . .] I'm appearing Thursday, one o'clock, courtroom No. 5. I'm done for. Everything is against me. Come, cher vieux, and let our friends know [. . .]

Erik Satie

On 12 July at the Court of First Instance of the Seine, Ricardo Viñes, Jean Cocteau, André Lhote, Gino Severini, Louis Durey, Léon Paul Fargue and Juan Gris testified in favour of Satie. Despite their support, Satie was condemned to a week in prison, a fine of a hundred francs and a thousand francs damages to Monsieur Poueigh. Maître Peytel gave notice of appeal.

Jean Cocteau to Misia Edwards

[13 July 1917]

[. . .] Poor Satie. Did anyone tell you we were all coming to you after the verdict? Satie didn't want to bother anyone beforehand, alas! He didn't think the matter was very serious. He was treated like an ignominious old imbecile. It was awful. And *L'Intransigeant* never misses a chance to be ignoble. What to do? If we could only keep him out of prison, because prison will discredit him with his pupils and in Arcueil [. . .]

Jean Cocteau

Guillaume Apollinaire to Misia Edwards

13 July 1917

[. . .] If Satie had called me to the Court I believe that in my presence Théry would not have dared to be as tough as he seems to have been by all the published accounts. But things go as they must and no doubt it will add greatness to Satie to have been jeered at, as all true artists have been at all times and in all places [. . .]

Guillaume Apollinaire

Satie accepted Ricardo Viñes's suggestion to spend a few days at the composer Déodat de Séverac's in the Pyrenees, to have a break.

Erik Satie to Ricardo Viñes

[Le Céret, July 1917?]

Mon brave ami,

I want to thank you vigorously: because of you I have escaped from a situation that was as dismal as it was disagreeable — I had too many newspapers against me, too many for one man.

Receive herewith your certificate as a good fellow; I give it to you in good heart.

Vôtre domestique et ami

E.S.

Sévérac added:

On the threshold of strict and proud Spain, fatherland of the great Viñes, his friends salute him.

Déodat de Sévérac

Back in Paris, Satie found himself in a most unpleasant situation. Very irritable, he quarrelled with everyone and in particular with Max Jacob, when he had gone to Jane Bathori's to hear one of the latter's poems set to music by Roland Manuel. Max Jacob gives an account of this stormy gathering in a letter to the couturier Jacques Doucet, a collector of contemporary autographs, who paid a few Parisian poets a salary on the sole condition that they wrote to him at least once a month.

Max Jacob to Jacques Doucet

10 August 1917

[. . .] Poor Satie! He arrived in a terrible state. They're killing him! They're cutting his throat! They're persecuting him! The publisher Rouart won't give him any more money because he's afraid Satie's royalties may be seized. The man who won the suit has the right to seize everything poor Satie possesses, including his scores etc. Satie will have a police record and won't be played in any publicly supported theatre. He won't have the right to travel, America is closed to him, Spain, who knows what else. . . In short, he feels that his life has been smashed, destroyed. Monsieur de Polignac asked him for the file on his case in order to pass it on to [the President of the French bar] Henri Robert, but he does nothing, in spite of his promises. Satie would have the possibility of a stay of proceedings if he appealed, but for that he would need a solicitor and a barrister and two thousand francs. I tried to reason with him, but he is suffering and wants to suffer. I quoted examples of great artists who went to prison without their life being destroyed, in short I've preached so many sermons in the name of common sense that he seems to have made me a scapegoat for his sufferings and he suddenly rushed off almost without shaking anyone's hand and without listening to Roland Manuel's music [. . .]

Max Jacob

Describing his sudden departure that day as a 'magic disappearance', Satie apologized to Roland Manuel in his own way.

Erik Satie to Roland Manuel

[August 1917]

Maybe I was a bit impulsive.

Too bad! Anyway, I feel no remorse.

So long as I don't have trouble with the police.

The police don't like disappearances; they don't understand anything about magic.

They'll put me in prison, an unhealthy prison, with no air, no distractions, no exercise. I shall be down and out and I shan't be living my life.

No doubt I shall fall sick; I'll have fleas, my back will be cold. I shan't be jolly. I shall develop a pot-belly and I'll be badly dressed.

No one will come to see me.

I'll probably stay there a very long time. I shan't be able to go to cafés or hunting, nor to my lawyer, nor on a bus, nor fishing at Montreuil, nor to the theatre, nor to the races, nor to the family bathing-beaches.

I shall lose all my contacts. How unlucky I am!

And then I shall have to choose a barrister, a good barrister who will ask for a lot of money.

What fun it is!

But . . . but . . . I have an alibi — a very-very little-ittle a-libi-bi, it seems to me: can't I say calmly that I was out of my wits and more than two thousand leagues from thinking I was committing a crime? That's a serious alibi; and how uncomplicated it is!

I'm saved!

Saved from bonds and bones stiffened by a stupid imprisonment!

I am my own saviour and I vote myself the thanks I deserve. In fact, I'm entitled to a fee of twenty-five francs.

I shall go and pick it up.

Waiter, my hat, my coat and my stick!

Erik Satie

While waiting to appear before the Appeal Court, Satie met Henri Robert, who promised to intervene on his behalf on condition that he apologize to the plaintiff.

At this period the composer was working on his 'symphonic drama' *Socrate*. Although depressed by Henri Robert's advice, he forced himself, in his turn, to drink his hemlock. On a page from a notebook in which he was copying out passages from Plato's *Dialogues* he drafted a letter of laborious explanations.

Erik Satie to Jean Poueigh

[10 September 1917]
You were justifiably offended & the malicious & unjustified insinuations of your articles had momentarily irritated me.

This incident is upsetting me to no purpose.

I had just spent ten months on the laborious task of *Parade*, months of legitimate exhaustion and strain . . . help me to defend myself, since I disapprove of the form. . .

Seeing that he would never be able to do what was asked of him, he broke off in the middle of a sentence and noted in a confident hand: 'Write H.R. that I refuse to apologize.' Then, on the next page in the same notebook he calmly started writing a hilarious text which he read publicly, under the title *Eloge des Critiques* [In Praise of Critics], at the Théâtre du Vieux Colombier on 5 February 1918, that is to say at the very moment when his most influential friends were trying to obtain a stay of execution of the first verdict which had been inexorably confirmed on appeal on 27 November 1917.

Here are some excerpts from his little speech:

Mesdames,
　　　　　Mesdemoiselles,
　　　　　　　　　Messieurs —
It is not by chance that I was made to choose this subject:
　　　　　　　　　'In Praise of Critics'
It is gratitude . . . . . for I am as grateful as I am gratified. . .

Last year I gave several lectures on 'Intelligence and Musicality among Animals'. . . .

Today I am going to speak to you about 'Intelligence and Musicality among Critics'. . . . .

. . . . . The subject is much the same, with some modifications, of course.

　　　　　　　. . . . .

　　　　　　　. . . . .

Friends have told me that this is a disagreeable subject. . . Why disagreeable?. . . There's no disagreement here, at least I don't see it. . . So I shall calmly deliver my praise of critics [. . .]

We don't know enough about critics; we don't know what they have done, what they are capable of doing. In a word, they are as misunderstood as animals, even though, like them, they have their usefulness [. . .] There are three sorts of critics: those of importance, those of less importance, those of no importance at all. The two latter kinds don't exist: all critics are important [. . .] An artist can be imitated; the critic is inimitable and invaluable. How could anyone imitate a critic? I ask myself. However, it would not be very interesting, not interesting at all: we have the original, that's enough for us [. . .] A critic's brain is a department store, a big department store. You can find everything there: artificial limbs, scientific instruments, bedding, arts supplies, travel rugs, a wide selection of furniture, French and foreign writing paper, articles for smokers, gloves, umbrellas, woollen goods, hats, sports goods, canes, optical products, perfumes etc. The critic knows everything, sees everything, says everything, hears everything, touches everything, moves everything, eats everything, confuses everything, and thinks none the less of it. What a man! Let us tell ourselves that!! [. . .] I have spent a lot of time studying the uses and customs of animals. Alas, they don't have critics! [. . .] The wolf doesn't criticize the sheep: he eats it. Not that he despises the sheep's art, but because he admires its flesh and even the bones of the woolly animal, which are so good in a stew.

We need a discipline of iron, or some quite different metal [. . .] We must not obey our evil passions, even if it is they themselves who order us to do so. By what can we recognize that passions are bad, as bad as the mange? Yes, by what?

By the pleasure we take in abandoning ourselves to them, in yielding to them, and by the fact that they displease the critics. They don't have any evil passions.

How could they, these good people? They have no passions at all, none. Always calm, they never think of anything but their duty of correcting the poor world's faults and earning a good living, so as to buy tobacco, quite simply [. . .]

On 15 March 1918, the Minister of the Interior finally approved probationary suspension of Satie's punishment, 'on condition of good conduct and not receiving any prison sentence during the next five years'.

CONTEMPORARIES

Satie demonstrated his own personal views on the critic's task in an article on Stravinsky which he wrote in 1922 for *Vanity Fair*. His approach was exceptionally modern clearly subordinating value judgement to strict information.

He stated his intentions elsewhere, in two letters to Stravinsky himself.

Erik Satie to Igor Stravinsky

Arcueil-Cachan 3 July 1922

Mon Cher Stravinsky —

Bonjour, Cher Ami. How are you?

[. . .] I have a great service to ask of you. It is this: A big American magazine has asked me to write an article on you. I hope you don't see any objections to that. This article has to be '*light and easy*' for the reader, while remaining fundamentally serious.

Would you be so kind as to send me:

— name and forename;

— birthplace;

— date of birth;

— your teachers (in order);

— a chronological list of your works (dates, where performed, publishers).

Indicate the main pamphlets, the most important articles written about you.

I am relying completely on you and ask you to please suggest what you *particularly* want me to say about you.

Send me all this as soon as possible, Cher Ami, I beg and implore you.

Amicalement vôtre:

Erik Satie

Erik Satie to Igor Stravinsky

Arcueil-Cachan, 9 August 1922

Mon Cher et Illustre Ami — It was kind of you to write me such a friendly no-note.

I haven't forgotten you because I'm working on the article about you every day.

I do not allow myself to judge you, not being a 'schoolmaster' like those I don't want to talk about: they are too stupid, poor fools. That's not surprising: on top of that they're idiots.

No, cher Ami, I do not pass judgement on you: I admire you and only talk about you as the great 'luminary' that you are. It would be impossible for me to confuse you with the 'wretched plodders' whom you know as well as I do. What miserable 'clods'! Yes.

I'll send you *Parade*.

Will you please convey my regards to Madame Stravinsky, Cher Ami.

Bien à vous, je suis

ES

Stravinsky said that he took to Satie at their first meeting. 'He's a sly one. He was full of guile and intelligently malicious.'

To increase the standing of Satie, who possessed the merit of having done *Parade* with him, Jean Cocteau, in his pamphlet *Le Coq et l'Arlequin*, had thrown a few darts at Stravinsky, towards whom he still nursed a grudge because of his refusal to collaborate on *David*. Satie hated this kind of comparison which in his view was entirely out of place. Using a formula close to that once thrown at

Picasso by Henri Rousseau *le Douanier* ('We are the greatest painters of this century: you in the Egyptian style, I in the modern style'), Satie said: 'Stravinsky is a magnificent bird and I'm a fish. Stravinsky isn't modern: he's a painter who uses violent colours, but his subjects are always classical and sometimes legendary'. 'It was nonsense', he explained, 'to compare birds to fishes.'

Similarly, in his article for *Vanity Fair*, before displaying his boundless admiration for Stravinsky, Satie made it clear that this did not imply any avowal of inferiority on his part.

I have always said — and I shall continue to repeat it long after I am dead — that there is no Truth in Art (no single Truth, that is).

The Truth of Chopin — that prodigious creator — is not the Truth of Mozart, that sumptuous musician whose *writing* is imperishably dazzling, just as Gluck's Truth is not Pergolese's any more than Liszt's Truth is Haydn's — which is just as well, after all.

If there is an artistic Truth, where does it begin: who is the Master who possesses it in its entirety? Is it Palestrina? Is it Bach? Is it Wagner?

To claim that there is a Truth in Art seems to me as strange, as astounding, as if I heard someone declare that there is a Locomotive Truth, a House Truth, an Aeroplane Truth, an Emperor Truth, a Beggar Truth and so on, and no one would dream — at least publicly — of expounding such a principle (out of modesty, perhaps, or out of simple commonsense); for we must not confuse a 'type' — even a *veritable*, *real* type — with Truth.

Nevertheless Satie once wondered out loud to Robert Caby: 'Compared with *Petrouchka*, does my little *Parade* stand up?' And he ended a third letter to his 'illustrious friend', with this playful declaration: 'I adore you: are you not the Great Stravinsky? I'm only the little Erik Satie'.

Before coming into contact with Stravinsky again in the entourage of the Ballets Russes, Satie had met him shortly after the creation of *Firebird*, at Debussy's.

This happened at a time when Satie's position in the musical life of Paris was beginning to improve and his relations with Debussy were suffering a parallel deterioration.

Erik Satie to Conrad Satie

27 March 1911

[. . .] I've just had a great success: the *Gymnopédies*, splendidly conducted by Debussy, were performed by the Cercle Musical Orchestra before an ultra-chic audience. It was very amusing. Because the concert consisted entirely of works by Claude, the *Gymnopédies* figured as orchestrated by him. I was afraid of hostility towards them. None at all. The 'Satistes' knew how to make themselves seen [. . .] Now there are 'Satistes'; they're no more fun than the 'Wagnerians', but they exist.

Odd![. . .]

Erik Satie

Satie and Debussy first met in the early 90's. 'From the moment I saw him for the first time,' said Satie, 'I was drawn to him and wanted to live constantly at his side.' He soon learned that this attraction was mutual. A copy of *Cinq Poèmes de Baudelaire* bears the dedication, dated 27 November 1892: 'To Erik Satie, gentle mediaeval musician who turned up in our century for the joy of his good friend Claude A. Debussy.'

During the ensuing years the links between them grew closer and closer. Debussy orchestrated two of the three *Gymnopédies*, the only work by another composer in which he ever took an interest, and Satie was so delighted by this move that he diligently copied out this orchestration in his finest handwriting, even accepting with good grace Debussy's suggestion to switch the titles of the first and third *Gymnopédie*.

It was better than an understanding, almost an idyll. And *Idylle* was indeed the title of a piece Satie dedicated to Debussy. A few fragments of their conversation are to be found in *Monsieur Croche antidilettante*. Whether he was living in Montmartre or Arcueil, Satie crossed Paris as often as possible — generally on foot — to see his friend.

Erik Satie to Conrad Satie

Arcueil, June 1901

[. . .] I am very much alone here. If I didn't have Debussy to talk to about things a bit above those common men discuss, I don't know what I should do to express my poor thoughts, if I do still express them.

The artists of our day are becoming businessmen and think the same way as a lawyer. One might even think they could give points to these latter — men, of course. It's no use my looking with my bad eyesight. I don't see a single gentleman around me.

It's not much fun. It seems to me young people are no longer the same, or at least no longer glorify the good and the beautiful.

Is this a misfortune? I ask myself this question trembling — enough on this subject; it puts me in a rage [. . .]

Erik Satie

At this period Satie was working on a composition he never managed to finish, *The Dreamy Fish*, 'music for a story by Lord Cheminot'. Satie would have liked Debussy to take a personal interest in this piece. As his friend was on holiday in Bichain with the parents of his first wife, Lily Texier, Satie wrote to remind him of this wish and at the same time to keep him informed about another work in progress, *Morceaux en forme de poire*. (The title was probably inspired by the dictionary definition of a spinning top. This 'pear-shaped object' actually 'spins round and round' as does the obsessive music of the *Morceaux*.)

Erik Satie to Claude Debussy

Arcueil, 17 August 1903

Mon bon Claude,

Monsieur Erik Satie wishes, with this note, to thank you for the pleasure he experienced in reading the one you addressed to him.

It is pleasant and profitable to correspond with you. As one might say: you return a hundredfold of what has been given you. When do you suppose, supposing precisely a supposition, that the two of you will return within our nice big walls (which will be beaten down like dogs, saving your respect)? It must be cold in the land of Bichain. The wind is perhaps fresher there than elsewhere; so you mustn't stay there for months and months, because you can catch nasty illnesses there, all worse in badness than is good for the health of the poor world.

And your pious and worthy Lady? Did you pass on my compliments to her? And this blasted dreamy fish? Did you make it take your hook? Monsieur Erik Satie is working at the present time on a delightful work entitled *2 Morceaux en forme de poire*. Monsieur Erik Satie is crazy about this new invention of his mind. He talks about it a lot and says very good things about it. He believes it superior to everything he has written up till now; perhaps he's wrong, but we mustn't tell him so: he wouldn't believe it.

You who know him well, tell him what you think about it; surely he will listen to you more attentively than to anyone, so great is his friendship for you. Do you want me to tell you? All right, through the moist mouth of this pen that speaks to you in my big old plebeian fingers the good language of good understanding which we supposedly owe each other I wish you good day, to you, mon bon Claude, to your Lady and to the honourable company here present, and please believe in the affective and affectionate affection of *vôtre vieux*

Erik Satie

When he wrote this letter, Satie had already received the shock of *Pelléas et Mélisande*, to his mind the perfect final

result of an aesthetic which he felt he had played a hand in developing. 'I must think up something else, or I'm done for', he is said to have remarked at that time. After *Morceaux en forme de poire*, which constitutes a kind of recapitulation of his work during the last ten years, he did, in fact, set out on a new road that was to distance him more and more from his favourite friend.

Erik Satie to Conrad Satie

Arcueil, 11 April 1911

[. . .] It's very kind of you to get hold of the things written about your old brother, who for so long was thought to be a madman. Don't you think that's odd? I would never have imagined anything like this could happen to me.

One person who isn't pleased is the good Claude. It's really his fault; if he had done sooner what Ravel — who makes no secret of the influence I had on him — has done, his position would be different.

Ravel — of whose works the Concerts Colonne gave a very important performance last Sunday — occupies a consider-able place in modern music. I knew him as a child and have always taken an interest in his work. I confess to my shame — that I didn't think him capable of publicly acknowledging that he owes me a lot. I was very moved by it.

Six years ago, Debussy married a very wealthy woman. He lives on the Avenue du Bois de Boulogne in a splendid mansion surrounded by a magnificent garden. He likes to invite me to lunch every Friday.

The success achieved by the *Gymnopédies* at the concert conducted by him at the Cercle Musical — a success which he did everything possible to turn into a failure — gave him an unpleasant surprise.

I'm not angry with him about it. He's the victim of his social climbing. Why won't he allow me a very small place in his shadow? I have no use for the sun. His conduct has turned against the 'Ravêlites' and the 'Satistes', people who have been keeping quiet in their place, but are now yelling at each other like polecats.

Chevillard (Concerts Lamoureux) didn't want to play the *Gymnopédies* in view of present trends. He will have to play some of my new things, he can't get out of that.

I'm imperturbably preparing some orchestral pieces. Ravel is orchestrating the *Préludes du 'Fils des Etoiles'* for performance at the advanced Concerts. You can see that the new season is looking good. We have nothing to complain about.

Ton frère: ES

Debussy had no doubt realized that this sudden promotion of Satie was not entirely innocent and that sooner or later it would be turned against himself. Embittered by illness, more and more isolated, anguished by the war which he could only watch powerlessly, Debussy, during his last years, allowed himself to make Satie pay, by incessant clumsy jests, for the role of 'precursor' that he had been made to play in spite of himself. At the moment when the wheel of fortune was finally about to turn in the right direction for him, Satie found himself denied the only approbation that really mattered to him. He could see only one solution: to stay away forever.

Erik Satie to Emma Debussy

Thursday 8 March 1917

Chère Madame — decidedly, it will be preferable if henceforth the 'Precursor' stays at home, far away.

Amicalement
ES

Painful teasing — and at the rehearsal yet! Yes. Quite unbearable, anyhow.

Erik Satie to Henry Prunières

Arcueil-Cachan, 14 Sept. 1917

Cher Monsieur et Ami — your card gave me the greatest pleasure. You speak to me of Debussy? I no longer see him.

Parade separated me from a great many friends. This work is the cause of many misfortunes. I have against me a thousand unpleasant people who have more or less abused and mistreated me. Too bad! [. . .] Come back soon. Here *prudhommisme* exists in a ferocious form. Vive Prudhomme. Roi Ubu.

It's charming! Amicalement vôtre: ES

Debussy died on 25 March 1918 while the cannon were thundering over Paris. Some twenty people were present at his funeral. Satie was not among them.

Several years later, Satie noted in his journal: 'When all is said and done, *ce bon* Debussy was something else again than all the others put together. . .'

And in 1920, when Henry Prunières (who had meanwhile become editor of *La Revue musicale*, born from the ashes of the *Revue musicale S.I.M.*) asked him to compose a work 'in memory of Debussy', he chose to set to music, 'in memory of a tender and admiring friendship of thirty years', these lines from Lamartine:

> Que me font ces vallons, ces palais, ces chaumières,
>   Vains objets dont pour moi tout charme est envole?
>   Fleuves, rochers, forêts, solitudes si chères,
>   Un seul être vous manque et tout est dépeuplé.

[What to me are these valleys, these palaces, these cottages/Vain objects from which for me all charm has been taken away?/Rivers, rocks, forests, solitude so dear,/A single being is lacking and everything is empty.]

SOCRATE

It has been said that Satie waited for Debussy's death before presenting his 'symphonic drama' *Socrate*, and it is indeed possible that concern not to occupy the same terrain as his friend delayed completion of a work which, for once, owes nothing to humour.

In any case, it was in the same letter in which he announced Debussy's death that Satie first spoke of *Socrate* to someone capable of writing about it and arranging a hearing.

Erik Satie to Henry Prunières

Arcueil-Cachan, 3 April 1918

Cher Monsieur et Ami — Thanks for your letter. Are you better? I hope so. There's nothing of special interest here, absolutely nothing.

You know of Debussy's death, of course. I wrote to him — fortunately for me — a few days before his death. Knowing that he was doomed, alas, I didn't want to remain on bad terms with him.

My poor friend! What a sad end. Now people will discover that he had enormous talent. That's life!

That's very true what you said about Casella. 'I don't like his music much because I find that in his work the form is generally lacking in sincerity and that he switches too easily from the style of Fauré to the style of Stravinsky.'

You are severe but just — although very indulgent, because you could have added that he is always lacking in intelligence. Is it intelligent to depict Latin visions with Slavic means; to confuse the sky of Italy with the sky of Russia; to dress Romans as Cossacks?

That's what our dear Casella does.

So you are indulgent towards this poor man — who isn't a good man, fortunately.

Before the war he seemed to be a pianist; since then he has proved that he never was. How will he play my music? Badly.

Excuse me, cher Ami, for writing to you on such paper: I'm in a café, quite a decent one, however.

When shall we see you? With the naked eye?

I'm working on a *Socrate* for the Princess de Polignac. My librettist is . . . Plato.

This work is coming along. Bathori sang a scrap of it to the Princess. It wasn't Russian, of course, nor was it Persian, nor Asian.

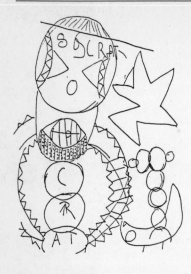

It's a return to classical simplicity with a modern sensibility. I owe this — very useful — return to my 'Cubist' friends. Bless them!

Bonjour, cher Ami, my regards to Madame Prunières.

Amitiés to Bébé, please?

ES

P.S. Thanks for putting me in your programme.

How will you describe me? I trust you of course.

What you say about Malipiero grieves me greatly.

It was the Princess Edmond de Polignac who had commissioned Satie to compose *Socrate* to be performed at one of her receptions. Stravinsky had composed *Renard* and Manuel de Falla *El Retablo de Maese Pedro* for this private salon, where the mistress of the house always reserved the one and only armchair in the front row for herself, while her selected guests were lined up some way behind her. The composer concerned was not always invited to the supper that followed the musical performance. He and his players were served refreshments in a separate room.

The widow of Prince Edmond de Polignac, née Winnaretta Singer, owed her considerable private income to the famous brand of sewing-machines. As she had studied ancient Greek, Satie's first idea was to compose a musical background to a reading of Plato's *Dialogues* to be performed by the Princess herself and one of her friends, Madame de Wendel, née Argyropoulos, in her Empire salon. He subsequently abandoned the idea of using the original language in favour of the French translation made, during the Second Empire, by the Academician Victor Cousin. He nevertheless retained the plan for a monochord chant evoking a reading by female voices, although the characters in this 'drama' were all male. He established his libretto himself by a skilful assemblage of extracts from the *Dialogues*.

'I have always wanted to do something on Socrates,'

Satie told Darius Milhaud. 'It's such an unjust story!' It was to the Greek philosopher that he would refer when wishing to express his admiration for the wise and limpid nature of one of his friends.

Erik Satie to Brancusi

Arcueil (France), 16 April 1923

Cher Bon Druid — how is your good old health, old friend?

People tell me you are a bit depressed. Is that true?

Since that's the way it is, I want to come over and say hello to you, you who are so kind — the best of men, like Socrates whose brother you must surely be.

You mustn't be too sad, dear good friend. We love you, you know.

Spit on the 'dumb-bells' day and night, you have every right, but don't forget you have friends who love and admire you, mon bon vieux. Yes. . .

Amicalement vôtre: ES

Inspired by Satie's 'symphonic drama', Brancusi sculpted a *Plato*, a *Socrates* and a *Socrates' Cup*. It has often been pointed out that the search for 'whiteness' and for essentials was common to both the sculptor and the composer.

In the small circle of Paris friends, Satie's choice of Socrates as the protagonist for this work automatically led to his being identified with him. After meeting Satie at Cocteau's, Paul Morand noted in his journal:

7 October 1916

Satie entered, resembling Socrates: his face is composed of two half moons; he scratches his goat's beard between each word. He doesn't talk about his genius, he tries above all to look sly. One can recognize in him the semi-failure, the man whom Debussy has always crushed and who still suffers from it. Satie is writing *Socrate* for the Princess de Polignac.

From the outset, Satie had been conscious of the challenge. He had confessed to Valentine Gross: 'I'm scared of failing with this work, which I want to be white and pure like the Antique. I'm all over the place and no longer know where to put myself. The fact is, something fine could be done with this idea, indeed!'

As at the time of *Parade*, Valentine was kept informed step by step of the development of the project.

Erik Satie to Valentine Gross

Arcueil-Cachan, 18 Jan. 1917

Chère Amie — I promised you an express letter: here it is. If it's late, that's not my fault, believe me. How are you? And the good Stern? Please give him my friendly greetings, and to you too, of course.

What am I doing? I'm working on the 'Life of Socrates'. I found a fine translation. Victor Cousin's.

Plato is a perfect collaborator, very gentle and never troublesome. It's a dream! I've written on this subject to the good Princess.

I'm swimming in happiness. At last, I'm free, free as air, as water, as the wild sheep. Long live Plato! Long live Victor Cousin! I'm free! Very free!

What happiness! I embrace you with all my heart.

You are my beloved big girl.

Your grandfather: ES

Since, for obvious reasons, he was physically absent, Plato did indeed appear to Satie an ideal collaborator, after the experience he had just been through with Cocteau, which had been utterly exasperating at times. So he did all he could to keep Cocteau from having any hand whatever in the new work. And in spite of Cocteau's efforts, and even tricks, to get to write at least the preface to the published score, this honour went to the poet René Chalupt, who had once composed a delicate text for a melody of Satie's, *Le Chapelier*, inspired by the Mad Hatter of *Alice in Wonderland*.

Erik Satie to René Chalupt

[1919]

Is your preface coming along? Short and to the point
[. . .] A clear summing up of what *Socrate* expresses. Its
significance in the art of music, its newness.

I'm asking of your friendship a piece of writing that is an
expression of pride.

State with authority without argument [. . .]

Erik Satie

Satie maintained the same proud and cutting tone on the
occasion of the first public performance of *Socrate*, put on
by the Société Nationale on 14 February 1920 at the Salle du
Conservatoire. 'Those who are unable to understand', we
read in the *Guide du Concert* over his signature, 'are
requested by me to maintain an attitude of complete
submission and inferiority'.

At this period, Satie had a solid reputation as a
humorist. So the audience greeted the philosopher's death
with wild laughter and critics went so far as to judge this
work 'one of the monuments of dry humour whose proper
place is in the pantheon of the Chat Noir'. Only one
Belgian pianist and musicologist, Paul Collaer, the future
founder and leading light of the Pro Arte concerts in
Brussels, showed himself sensitive to the emotional charge
emanating from this austere work.

Erik Satie to Paul Collaer

Arcueil-Cachan — Seine, 16 May 1920

Cher Monsieur (permit me to use the epithet 'cher': you
deserve it) — Poulenc has sent me your article on *Socrate*.

How much I thank you for what you have written about
my score! I read this 'talk' with great joy: it proves that there
are good people in the world.

Thank you, Cher Monsieur; thank you. In writing *Socrate* I
thought I was composing a simple work, without the least
idea of conflict; for I am only a humble admirer of Socrates
and Plato — who look like two charming gentlemen.

When performed at our Conservatoire by the Société Nationale, my music was badly received, which didn't surprise me; but I was surprised to see the audience laugh at Plato's text. Yes.

Strange, isn't it?

Bonjour, Cher Monsieur; I hope that we shall meet before long.

Erik Satie

P.S. People seem to believe that the great Socrates is a character invented by me — and this in Paris!

At a private performance of *Socrate*, which brought the 'Tout Paris' of arts and letters to Adrienne Monnier's Maison des Amis des Livres on 21 March 1919, the reaction was different. An audience that included among others Gide, Fargue, Paul Valéry and James Joyce applauded the singer Suzanne Balguerie accompanied by the composer. Later Gertrude Stein became a devotee of Satie's when she heard Virgil Thomson play and himself sing *Socrate* in his Paris garret. For this work Alexander Calder designed in 1936 his first work for the theatre: a mobile which, for the first time, was made to move naturally, under simple air pressure, instead of employing machinery. In 1944 John Cage made a transcription of *Socrate* for two pianos, for which Merce Cunningham choreographed the first movement under the title *Idyllic Song*. Cage also made use of *Socrate* in his composition *Cheap Imitation*, submitting it to I Ching chance operations. It was for *Socrate* that Merce Cunningham conceived his choreography *Second Hand*.

Today *Socrate* is almost universally considered a high point in Western music of the 20th century.

MASKED BALLS

In the late summer of 1918, without waiting for the end of the war, Count Etienne Bonnin de la Bonnetière de Beaumont and his wife, Countess Edith de Taisne de Beaumont, opened their salon in the rue Duroc. Since the state of war had promoted contacts between high society and others (at the front, and in Montparnasse) it now appeared quite natural that the Beaumonts should invite a few artists to their receptions, something that would have been unheard of in the past.

Jean Cocteau, who had shared life in the trenches, or rather behind the lines, with Beaumont, now served as a liaison officer between the two worlds.

On being invited to this first historic evening Satie, who was going through one of his worst moments of loneliness and distress, did not have the courage to take part.

Erik Satie to Etienne de Beaumont

24 August 1918

Cher Ami & Bon Monsieur,

How very sorry I am not to be able to come and hear those fine fellows: I am busy.

You are really too kind to have thought of me and to have invited me so cordially.

Bonjour, cher Monsieur & Ami, forgive me, please, and a thousand times thank you.

ES

Back in Paris, having got over his experience with the ambulances, Etienne de Beaumont had immediately devoted himself to another innovation, the creation of a Franco-American committee for aid to artists. Satie was one of the first to benefit from these good works.

Erik Satie to Mrs G.M. Tuttle, New York

Arcueil-Cachan, 5 November 1918

Madame — Mr Blair-Fairchild informed me that it was to you that I owed — owe — the gracious aid which he conveyed to me through the good offices of the Franco-American Committee of the Conservatoire (of Paris).

It was very good of you, Madame, to have done for me what you have been so kind as to do, & I thank you with all my heart.

I regret not having been able to do it earlier (to thank you) — as I told Mr Blair-Fairchild. Will you forgive me, Madame, for this delay?

I had flu so badly that I was incapable of writing anything whatever. I couldn't eat; I couldn't drink; I couldn't laugh — or only with one eye; I couldn't dance; I looked like a shadow, but an unpleasant and sorrowful shadow. I could no longer recognize myself & it happened several times that I took myself for someone else.

My sickness greatly amused my doctor. I became horribly ugly, but — fortunately — with a comical and most entertaining ugliness. That's what my doctor tells me. Now I'm saved & to guard against a recurrence of the illness, I constantly carry with me a solid lifebelt on the advice of my druggist — a whimsical man.

Forgive me, Madame, for bothering you with such confidential details.

Please allow me to thank you once more for your kindness and please accept the respectful salutations of him who signs himself

Erik Satie

On Wednesday 2 April 1919 Satie was engaged by
Beaumont, for a fee, to play his *Morceaux en forme de poire*
with André Salomon at a reception in honour of Queen
Mary of Romania. Pierre Bertin, who was one of the
guests that evening (or one of the performers? history does
not tell us), describes his entry thus:

> With two fingers on his mouth as always, Erik Satie
> crossed the room, headed for the Queen and chatted
> with her for a long time. When he withdrew, everyone
> asked him curiously what the Queen had said to him.
> Erik Satie replied gravely: 'The Queen told me I have a
> fine old man's head'.

Erik Satie to Edith de Beaumont

Arcueil-Cachan, 4 April 1919
Chère Comtesse & Exquise Dame —
Forgive me for writing to you on paper like this — I have
nothing else at hand.
Here is the address of André Salomon: 58 rue Demours,
58, Paris — XVIIe.
How nice it was on Wednesday! The Queen is delightful. I
was very happy.
Thank you with all my heart. A thousand good wishes to
Monsieur de Beaumont.
Respectueusement vôtre je suis, Madame,

Erik Satie

Friday [11 April 1919]
Chère Bonne Comtesse — I thank you for your kind
remittance: . . . it did not fall on deaf ears. Thank you forever
and ever.
Please give my good wishes to Monsieur de Beaumont.
Bonjour, chère bonne Comtesse, from your respectful &
devoted

Erik Satie

Having always had a weakness for entertainments, Etienne de Beaumont organized a masked ball every year. In *Le Bal du Comte d'Orgel* Raymond Radiguet describes one of these evenings typical of Parisian high society, whose greatest passion, he notes, was to 'put on a disguise'.

Radiguet made no secret of the fact that Anne d'Orgel was intended to be a portrait of Count de Beaumont. 'But Count d'Orgel,' he commented, 'is much better.'

Satie took part in the Beaumont balls. According to Maxime Jacob he even used 'to get furious if his domino was less elegant than Léon Paul Fargue's'. The guests' costumes were supposed, in principle, to be inspired by a theatrical theme laid down each year by the master of the house. In 1923 the theme was 'Antiquity under Louis XIV', in memory, no doubt, of a famous pre-war masked ball given by Paul Poiret to illustrate Lully's *Festes de Bacchus*. This time Satie was even more directly involved, since he was asked to compose the music for a *tableau vivant* to be presented in the course of the evening under the direction of Léonide Massine, a deserter from the Ballets Russes temporarily out of work. No doubt dissatisfied with the choreography of *Parade* (even though this was regarded by everyone — beginning with Cocteau, who claimed to be the true inspirer — as profoundly innovative), Satie suggested to Beaumont that he should not write his score until after Massine had designed the movements of the characters. This procedure, he confided to the painter Moïse Kisling, was the only way he could protect himself from being misinterpreted.

Erik Satie to Edith de Beaumont

[23 March 1922]

Chère & Exquise Comtesse — I telephoned you yesterday. Your express letter reached me at two in the morning as I got home. I'm extremely sorry.

There's nothing I'd like better than to work with Massine.

At Derain's all three of us talked about this 'initial' choreography: starting off with the choreographer, which is very 'new' and has never been done before.

I'm the one who suggested this idea to Massine.

How sorry I am not to have been able to come!. . .

Mille choses au bon Comte, je vous prie.

Respectueusement: Erik Satie

The Beaumonts' music room, full of gilded woodwork, was dominated by a magnificent organ, built to special order. Satie decided to write a score for this instrument, despite the reservations expressed by Cocteau who, this time, had not permitted himself to be left out. The *Parade* team was reassembled in its entirety when Picasso agreed to design the costumes, as he had done for another of the Beaumonts' balls, the *Bal des Jeux*. The former ballerina from the Ballets Russes, Olga Koklova, who had meanwhile become Madame Pablo Picasso, was to play a part in the *tableau*, involving several characters, which was ultimately to be entitled *La Statue retrouvée* (the discovered Statue) but which for the time being was called *Divertissement*.

Erik Satie to Edith de Beaumont

Arcueil-Cachan, 26th Dec. 1922

Chère Exquise Comtesse — The good Count & you must be thinking very badly of me.

Believe me, it isn't my fault: various events have kept me far from the things I love. . . The *Divertissement* is one of those things — that I love & adore. Yes.

I'm very surprised to see that Jean shares the prejudice of the masses against the organ. . . Odd, isn't it?. . . Yes.

I very much hope to win him over to our cause — our good cause. Yes.

The organ isn't necessarily religious & funereal, good old instrument that it is. Just remember the gilt-painted merry-go-round. Well?. . .

Souvenir amical à tous deux: Erik Satie

Arcueil-Cachan, 31 Dec. 1922

Chère Délicieuse Comtesse — I couldn't come over to say hello to you this afternoon, & I beg you to forgive me.

Please accept here my good wishes for the New Year to you & the good Count.

Is the organ all right? I must come over and 'turn it inside out' — just to see what there is inside. Perhaps he is a ventriloquist, the good old instrument.

Jean gave me a good idea concerning it (the *Divertissement*). Yes.

It's not stupid, you'll see.

Mille choses au bon Comte, s'il vous plaît; et croyez moi, chère Comtesse, vôtre tout dévoué   Erik Satie

Arcueil, 22 March 1923

Chère Exquise Comtesse — A thousand good mornings & good nights. I have just seen the Picassos myself — Dame & Monsieur. I couldn't get to see them earlier:. . . they weren't free.

I talked to them about the *Divertissement*. They want to take part in it, but tell me they haven't heard anything about it from *you*. . . What's happened?. . . A mistake, no doubt. . . I was counting on you to bring us together with some ladies from the choreography. Don't abandon the idea, I beg you . . . let's have everything arranged before you leave, if possible.

Amitiés au bon Comte, n'est-ce pas? & veuillez agréer, Chère Comtesse, mes salutations respectueuses   ES

Erik Satie to Etienne de Beaumont

Arcueil, 28 April 1923 (or rather 27 April)

Cher Très Bon Comte — Delighted to see you again, you & the exquisite Countess. Yes.

Sure, we must see each other & as soon as possible too!

I've seen Massine (he's very stupid, our dear friend, & very much a dancer. Yes.) about Madame Picasso. But the

Marquise de Médicis? And the other pretty Lady? (I know there's nothing she would like better than to be one of us). Yes.

Monday at 12:30 will be fine. We will chat.

Bien à vous: ES

One of the performers in *La Statue retrouvée* was Daisy Fellowes, the niece of the Princess Edmond de Polignac, a colourful character used to giving the newspapers something to talk about. Satie valued this performer highly, she had 'gumption'. In addition, he composed for the same evening a vocal number for the 'angelic voice' of Madame René Jacquemaire, née Marguerite di Pietro and known familiarly as Ririte. This latter, who was the daughter of Jeanne Lanvin, was destined, after her second marriage to Count Jean de Polignac, to become a pillar of the Parisian salons under the name of Marie-Blanche de Polignac. This new forename was doubtless inspired by a family story: one of Ririte's ancestors, the sweet Blanche Lanvin, had been a mistress of Victor Hugo.

Erik Satie to Edith de Beaumont

Arcueil, 14 May 1923

Chère Exquise Comtesse — This time we've done it. On Thursday the Jacquemaire number (the most complicated) will be finished. I simply couldn't get to the end of it. Yes.

From Friday on I shall be at the disposal of the dancers. We shall be ready, have no fear as far as my work is concerned.

Are you well? And the good, dear Count? Please give him my best wishes, Madame.

It would be very kind of you to see the Picassos. And his costumes? We're getting on to serious matters now. Yes.

We must keep a weather eye open.

Bonjour, Chère Exquise Comtesse: see you soon, surrounded by orchestras & sounds. Yes.

ES

The Jacquemaire number — 'the most complicated' — consisted of five minuscule melodies, the *Ludions*, set to poems by Léon Paul Fargue. One of the poems, *Air du Rat*, had been written by Fargue at the age of ten.

On 29 May, at final rehearsal, Fargue noticed that his name had been omitted from the programme and lost his temper both with Satie — who was doubtless not responsible for this oversight — and with the Count de Beaumont. In his annoyance, Beaumont talked about challenging the poet to a duel. 'All right,' replied Fargue, 'but since I'm the offended party I have the right to choose the weapons, and I choose spelling.'

Fargue had known Satie since the time when they both lived with their respective parents, in the north of Paris. Apart from the pleasure of playing with words, they shared a common taste for night-time strolls and frequent visits to booksellers and the Jardin des Plantes. According to Adrienne Monnier, who often received them together in her Maison des Amis des Livres, Satie was to Fargue 'what the Tashi Lama is to the Dalai Lama'. In order to get the exact measure of this evaluation, however, we must bear in mind that, for Adrienne Monnier, Fargue was the absolute master of thought.

The quarrel that occurred at the Beaumonts' was to put an end to all contact between Fargue and Satie. 'As usual in Fargue's feuds,' Adrienne Monnier's great friend Sylvia Beach reports, 'he spent a good deal of time and took a lot of trouble to write the most dreadfully insulting things he could think of in daily letters to Satie. Not satisfied with mailing them in Paris, he would go all the way to Arcueil-Cachan, where Satie lived, to slip another insulting letter under his door. Even the final one, too outrageous to repeat, failed to get anything but a laugh from Satie, a mild, philosophically-minded man, the composer, after all, of *Socrate*, and I think that was the last shot fired.'

When Satie fell ill, Fargue refused to go and see him in the hospital despite the insistence of the publisher Lerolle,

who wanted to publish the *Ludions*. Nor did he attend his
old friend's funeral. Without ever drawing his portrait, as
he did with other exceptional personalities he had known,
Fargue nevertheless several times refers to Satie in his
book as 'a true master, the inventor of *musique maisonnière*
[household music]'.

The fashion, started by the Beaumonts, of mixing artists
with princesses was soon followed by other society people.
However, under such circumstances the position of the
artists remained ambiguous. Their benefactors did not
rest content with their presence, their conversation, the
prestige of their names, but above all demanded — with a
financial inducement, of course — their active participation. The painters were set to work designing the setting
for receptions, while the poets were required to read their
poems and the composers to play their works, as in the
grand days of the King. Thus every head of a household
could imagine that he had his own little private Versailles.
We have only to read a page from the journal of Princess
Ghika to see that the presence of a few artists, even if they
enjoyed international reputations, ultimately carried no
more weight than the elegance of the dresses and the
profusion of the jewellery.

Princess Georges Ghika, née Anne-Marie Chassaigne,
was better known under the name Liane de Pougy which
she had once rendered famous by displaying her charms
at the Folies Bergère. Having become a Tertiary
Dominican at the end of her life, she died as Sister
Anne-Marie.

From the Journal of Princess Ghika
                    Roscoff, Clos Marie, 5 July 1922
Our life chez Pépé was nothing but joy, pleasures,
festivities and banquets [. . .] The servants were
perfect, our first reception magnificent [. . .] Nathalie
[Barney] came, the Countess Clauzel, Madame de
Lubersac, the Countess de La Béraudière, the most

famous actresses [. . .] In short, there were seventy of us and we had a lot of fun looking, gossiping, patting ourselves on the back, tippling. Pépé received the guests in the large salon, assisted by the Baroness de l'Epée, and they were brought to me in the little red salon adjacent to the dining room where the enormous buffet was laid out [. . .]

We had three musicians: Auric, Poulenc and Erik Satie. They played their works [. . .]

I wore my peplum from Madeleine Vionnet's in black crêpe-georgette, a unique, wonderful thing, such a success that it's beyond words [. . .]. There were simply endless strings of pearls! Madame Marthe Besnuth, the fiancée of Prince Coloradi-Mansfeld alone wore three million's worth [. . .].

These society evenings were obviously very exclusive. Not to be a part of them could be a disaster for an ambitious young man.

Just as mixing with the princesses was not open to just anyone, so people who did not have 'blue blood' could not hope to receive society in their homes. Society people were the first to regret this, because they were ready to seize any opportunity for amusement if they could do so without damaging their reputations.

Amphibious by nature, curious about all and gifted with the faculty of slipping in anywhere, 'like a draught of air', Jean Cocteau was well acquainted with this situation and knew how to turn it to his advantage at times. In order to get the eccentric dancer Caryathis off to a good start, on the occasion of her first dance recital, he suggested that she should give a masked ball at which the guests could maintain their anonymity. He undertook, under these conditions, to bring the finest names in Paris to her home.

The centrepiece of Caryathis' performance was to be a suite of dances, *La Belle Excentrique*, specially composed by Erik Satie. While refusing to take part in this ball himself, Satie thought it a very amusing idea and even volunteered to act as adviser.

Erik Satie to Caryathis

[June 1921]

Chère Grande Artiste, exquise amie, you're a good egg! Of course I love your company.

I'll come on Thursday, if it suits you, to lunch under the big oak in your garden. The fountain will be obligatory. In this terrible heat my skin is so sensitive [. . .]

ES

'The fountain,' Caryathis relates, 'was nothing more than my watering hose which I hooked onto the tree with the jet thrown onto the wall; like this Satie, who used to be very flushed after the numerous aperitifs or the champagne with the meal, found the reflected rays of the sun pleasant.

'He drew up a plan of how the masked ball should proceed. A loudspeaker, he told me, would add to the excitement. Once all these social treasures were gathered together, the speaker would broadcast in the language of the greatest artists of all times, which would unleash a battle of pride. Thus every mask would be thrown to the wind. . .'

That evening Caryathis put on the dress made for her performance, the design of which had greatly concerned Satie. Before reaching a choice he had made the rounds of the painters and dressmakers in the company of the dancer:

Van Dongen put him off by his mercenary spirit; at Poiret's we had scarcely seen three dresses when he turned to me. Out of the corner of his mouth he let slip two words: "Harem stuff!" Before Marie Laurencin's model, he grew irritable. "No, no! To hell with charm!" His reaction to Jean Hugo's model was more positive. "But my music calls for something outrageous," he said. "A woman who is more like a zebra than a doe."

It was once again Cocteau who resolved the problem by designing, in no time at all, a 'costume for a mad American woman from the Salvation Army out for revenge'. At Caryathis' masked ball Cocteau appeared in the Mercury costume he always wore on such occasions: dressed in grey tights and a winged helmet, carrying Mercury's wand and moving with great rapidity,

> he glided through the ground floor, the two upper floors and the ballroom. The guests parted as he moved among them in order to get a better look at him. He seemed to be flying, and not thanks to the wings on his heels and his helmet: his joy went out beyond those present, he was drawn to some horizon like an arrow seeking its target.

Cocteau had always felt a deep affinity for the mythological figure of Mercury and everything it represented, so it was not without malice that Satie and Picasso chose this character for a ballet conceived at a time when Satie had finally and noisily broken with Cocteau, whom he considered, among other things, as responsible for having led Poulenc and Auric astray.

Having discovered through his masked balls that he could get a certain number of stars from the Ballets Russes to perform for him, the Count de Beaumont told himself that a single step more would place him on the same footing as Diaghilev. So he hired a theatre, the Cigale music-hall, chose for his enterprise the fetching title *Soirée de Paris*, identical but for one letter with Apollinaire's famous revue *Soirées de Paris*, and commissioned a series of ballets and plays from the artists and poets who frequented his house. Apart from Picasso, Satie and Massine, Darius Milhaud, Henri Sauguet, Roger Désormière, Marie Laurencin, Valentine and Jean Hugo, Paul Morand and André Derain were also mobilized, and so were Tristan Tzara (associated rather surprisingly with an ageing Loïe Fuller) and, of course, Jean Cocteau, who

this time was to present his own version of *Romeo and Juliet*. Most of these ballets and plays took shape in the course of long confabulations at the *Boeuf sur le Toit* cabaret, which had taken its name from a 'farce' by Cocteau and Milhaud, performed by the Fratellini brothers, some years earlier in a *Concert-Spectacle* financed by the Count de Beaumont.

Satie and Picasso were the first to set to work. Delighted not to have any intermediary between himself and the painter this time, Satie composed directly from the drawings as they progressed. The subject, *Les Aventures de Mercure*, was kept secret for a long time. Satie told everyone he didn't know what it was himself, claiming that when Beaumont commissioned the music from him he had refused to tell him the scenario 'in order to keep it as a surprise'. Had not Apollinaire said that 'the surprise effect' was essential to the Esprit Nouveau? This joke was doubtless intended by Satie as an allusion to the farce *Le Boeuf sur le Toit*, the scenario for which Cocteau had actually written to pre-existent music by Milhaud — and only, it was whispered, after the tickets had been sold. In the case of *Mercure*, on the contrary, it is far more likely that it was really the Count de Beaumont who did not know what Picasso and Satie were cooking up, to wit the description — on the pretext of being inspired by Greco-Roman mythology — of the method of producing alchemical gold, a topic regarded as heretical and hence taboo at that time.

In addition, a scene from the ballet, entitled *Les Festes de Bacchus*, contained an allusion to the masked ball of the same title once given by Paul Poiret, a subtle way for Picasso and Satie to pleasantly tease Etienne de Beaumont, whose ambition it was to equal Poiret and Diaghilev both at the same time.

Satie composed his score in two months, delivering it to the Count de Beaumont a bit at a time as it progressed in return for small sums of money (a proper contract was not drawn up until after the first performances). This system

of piecemeal payment which, on the one hand covered his most immediate living expenses, on the other prevented him from squandering his whole fee in one day — as had happened in the past. But incomplete deliveries of a work in progress was certainly not the ideal method for the choreographer Léonide Massine nor for Roger Désormière, a member of the Ecole d'Arcueil, who on this occasion was making his début as conductor.

Erik Satie to Léonide Massine

Monday, 7 April 1924

Cher Ami — Don't worry. I'm finishing Part Two — which I will bring you on Wednesday . . . I can't possibly go any faster, mon cher Ami: I can't hand over to you work which I couldn't defend. You who are conscience personified will understand me. . . In any case, I think I shall have finished the whole composition by the 15th (*a week from tomorrow*). . . .

Please remember me to the good Countess and the good Count, please.

Bien vôtre je suis: ES

Tuesday, 15 April 1924

Cher Grand Artiste — Bonjour.

I've finished the 'Polka', the 'New Dance' and 'The Apparition of Chaos' (*slightly ironic:* after all, Chaos itself is pretty comical). I've started the Finale (*Abduction of Proserpine*) for the third time. Dammit!. . . I had to. . .

You'll have the ending (*Terminus*) on Thursday. Yes.

Are you well? Everyone is fairly well. What weather!. . . It's incredible.

Please remember me kindly to the 'exquisite Countess'.

Amitiés to the good Count and to yourself by   ES

Sunday, 4 May 1924

Cher Grand Artiste — Tomorrow you will have the rest of the orchestration (the whole of Part Two).

Can you let me have the 'fair copy' of the piano score? I need it urgently in order to go ahead with my work. This 'fair copy' is the whole of Part Three.

I am astounded by what you so kindly showed me of your splendid choreography. Yes.

Till tomorrow (around noon). I'll drop in to say hello if you're at rue Duroc.

Bon souvenir to the 'exquisite Countess' & to the good Count.

Bien vôtre: ES

Erik Satie to Etienne de Beaumont

Saturday, 10 May 1924

Cher Bon Comte — Came yesterday Friday to bring you the end of the adaptation of *Mercure*. I didn't leave the manuscript because I didn't find anyone in charge I could safely give it to. I came back this afternoon. You couldn't receive me.

My work is finished.

Bien a vous: ES

Erik Satie to Roger Désormière

Sunday 11 May 1924

Cher Ami — Bonjour. How're things? I've finished the whole orchestration of the *Aventures de Mercure* last Friday. Great!. . .

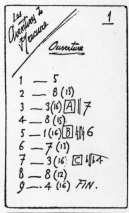

I've been to the rue Duroc several times to deposit this last part, but I couldn't leave it, since I didn't find anyone in charge to give it to. Anyway, I want to give it into the hands of the good Count (*himself*), (*for reasons of an economic nature of the most monetary kind*). Yes.

If you need this ending (to have copies made), will you *please* address yourself, as soon as possible, to the said Count. Yes.

Long life to the *Ecole d'Arcueil*! Yes!

ES

The première of *Mercure* on 16 June 1924 took place in a hostile atmosphere. The friends of Diaghilev, with Misia at the head, and Satie's old and new enemies did their best to ruin the performance. Nevertheless, after the composer's death, *Mercure* was to have the distinction of being the only ballet Diaghilev bought ready-made. The director of the Ballets Russes, however, only presented it once in Paris and a second time in London, where he did not even inform the press, because he feared negative reactions in the face of the originality of Picasso's scenery (he had audaciously mingled the dancers with moving wooden and wickerwork puppets, creating, in Gertrude Stein's words, 'pure calligraphy').

Despite the splendour of a repertoire made up of perfectly integrated creations all signed with prestigious names, *Soirée de Paris* did not bring in the public, who had been put off by written and verbal news reports. The most malicious gossip was making the rounds. In Paris salons, for example, the rumour circulated that in order to help her son, who was henceforth known as the 'current (ac)Count', Etienne's mother had one evening bought up all the seats in the theatre but had then forgotten to hand them out, so that they had played that evening to an empty house. . .

Erik Satie to Rolf de Maré

Sunday 29 June 1924

Mon cher Directeur — Don't worry: I'm working for you. It's going all right. . .

The Cigale (Beaumont) has closed its doors. . . This poor Count — who is, after all, a good man — instead of compliments has only received insults and other nice things. . . That's life! Most consoling!

Mille choses to Börlin & to yourself from

ES

Soirée de Paris was over. The following year, the Count de Beaumont returned to masked balls.

FURNITURE MUSIC

The bomb blast of *Parade* had made itself heard even outside the frontiers of France and very specially in those places sheltered from non-metaphorical bombs, where the dynamiters of art were waiting for the end of a war that did not concern them. Considered as potential allies, the names of the authors of this ballet — Satie, Picasso and Cocteau — began to appear in such reviews as *Dada*, published in Zurich by Tzara, and *391*, established in Barcelona by Picabia and then transferred first to New York and then to Zurich, before finally running aground in Paris. Incorrectly spelt — which suggests a still superficial contact between the persons concerned — the name of *Erick Satye* also figures in the 'message poster' *Mouvement Dada* conceived by Picabia in 1919 as a kind of map of the most significant artistic trends of the day.

The Zurich Dadas did not confine themselves to annexing Satie (with or without his consent?) but also played his music. In his account of a Dada evening that took place on 9 April 1919 in the Kaufleuten Saal, Tristan Tzara — who described himself on this occasion as the 'acrobat tamer' — reports that Suzanne Perrottet played 'Erik Satie (+ recitations), a musical non-music irony of don't give a damnism, the crazy kid on the miracle ladder of the Dada Movement'. Satie continued to be played at Dadaist manifestations in Paris and elsewhere. A *Ragtime Dada* — which is nothing else than the 'Ragtime' from

Parade — appears on the posters for the tour organized by Schwitters and Van Doesburg in the Netherlands in 1923.

When the war ended, the Dadas left Zurich for Paris, where they found themselves confronted by a much more complex situation than they had imagined. Their natural link was with the review *Littérature* (edited by Aragon, Breton and Soupault) which in fact played in Paris a role comparable to that played elsewhere by *Dada* and *391*. The editors of *Littérature* were also habitués of Adrienne Monnier's Maison des Amis des Livres, who were beholden to the mandarins of the *Nouvelle Revue Française*, Gide, Fargue, Valéry, Jean Paulhan. . . More sensitive to the aura of the *N.R.F.* than their rebellious attitude would have led one to believe, these ambitious young lions quickly assimilated the idiosyncrasies of their elders and hence, just like them, hated a figure like Cocteau, who had long been struggling in vain to gain entry into this closed circle. Being the first to arrive in Paris, Picabia immediately informed Tzara — who stayed on in Zurich for a few months — of these false notes.

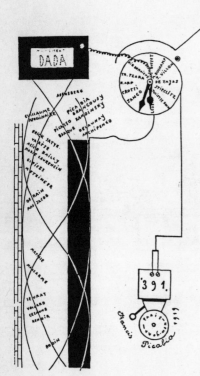

Francis Picabia to Tristan Tzara

Friday, 28 March 1919

Mon cher Tzara [. . .] There's nothing happening in Paris, silly gossip, all the geniuses spend their time quarrelling with each other and then making up [. . .] Picasso is more and more admired by everyone, being the most 'arrivé' — where he's arrived I don't know, but those who admire him know [. . .] Jean Cocteau is on very bad terms with everyone. Erik Satie calls him an idiot and all the others a parasite, so you can see what a delightful life we can live here [. . .] I'd have loved to see your evening in Zurich: we'll do one here, come quick [. . .]

Très affecteusement vôtre

Francis Picabia

In fact when Tzara arrived in Paris the high jinks began. Under his impetus, performances multiplied. Although

the review *Littérature* lent its imprint to these performances, the public automatically equated all the partici-
pants with Dada. In that year, 1920, the Group of Six,
which had just been born, figured as the viable
avant-garde. So, along with Satie's, it was the music of the
'Six' that was regularly played at the *Littérature* Fridays,
despite the objections raised in some quarters to
'Cocteau's gang'. Getting hold of the wrong end of the
stick, certain newspapers went so far as to see in Cocteau
the leader of the Dadas. . . For his part, Cocteau did his
best to increase the confusion by publishing a review, *Le
Coq*, whose typography was inspired by that of *391* and
Dada.

The Dadaists defended themselves as best they could.
While continuing to use the music of Satie and the Six at
their performances, they did not hesitate to publish
denigrations in their pamphlets. Thus we can read in *Z*
this unflattering phrase: 'Auric Satie with the Cocteau
nut' (a pun on Erik Satie, coconut and the expression *à la
noix*, 'not up to much') and in *Dadaphone* the following
ill-natured banter: 'Satie invented Furniture Music as a
means of getting into society (rented out for a party)'.

And yet this Furniture Music, at which the official
Dadaists jeered, was undoubtedly the only musical
manifestation of the period that is truly Dadaist in spirit.

Although the radio had not yet become common, it was
evident that people increasingly liked to carry out their
day-to-day activities against a musical background. To
satisfy this growing need, and at the same time to protect
music that called for a more attentive hearing from this
casual attitude, Satie conceived the idea of providing an
appropriate consumer product. So on 8 March 1920,
during the intermissions of a play by Max Jacob staged
at the Galerie Barbazanges by Pierre Bertin, he launched
this 'utilitarian music', which was emphatically not to be
listened to. A few fragments by the composers he hated the

most, Ambroise Thomas and Camille Saint-Saëns, were mingled in his score which five instruments, scattered about the hall, were instructed to repeat 'ad lib, no more'. Durey thought this idea *une aimable gaminerie*, an agreeable child's prank. Auric later declared that he considered it an 'irritating delusion'. Alone of the Six, Milhaud played an enthusiastic part in it.

Erik Satie to Pierre Bertin

Arcueil-Cachan, 1 March 1920

Cher Ami — Along with me, Milhaud is making Furniture Music. He has stunning ideas. Tell us — him and me — the time of the Sunday rehearsal.

We shall go with *three* clarinets and *one* trombone — Let Delgrange know.

Please put Milhaud's name on the programmes — You must ask Cocteau to take part. We *must* have him with us.

Amicalement à vous: Erik Satie

Erik Satie to Darius Milhaud

Friday, 5 March 1920

Cher Milhe-Milhe — This is Tie-Tie writing to you: he has finished his two 'things'. He's as happy as a king.

We'll 'get the better of them'. Have you read *Comoedia*? I'm 'flabbergasted' by that article. Yes, very.

They talk about the 'mysterious collaborator': 'one of the most gifted young composers of the new school — but, ssh, it's a surprise!' Who is it?

How I thank you for coming to the 'Furniture Music.' Yes, old fellow.

On Sunday, right?

Please remember me kindly to your mother and father.

Votre vieil ami:

Erik Satie

P.S. Poor Auric!

At the Galerie Barbazanges, however, Satie did not
achieve the result he had expected. Although invited to
'walk about, eat, drink', the audience remained respectfully seated. Milhaud recounts: 'It was no use Satie
shouting: "Talk, for heaven's sake! Move around! Don't
listen!" They kept quiet. They listened. The whole thing
went wrong'.

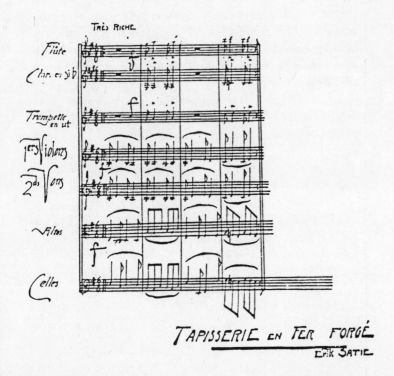

PSEUDO-DADAS

Little by little Satie's relations with the Paris Dadas — or at least with some of them — nevertheless improved, as is indicated by the amiable pun, 'Erik is Satierik', which Picabia published in the November 1920 issue of *391*. Satie was even invited to contribute to this review. He then submitted some of his '*pensées*'. It must be admitted in this connection that with Picabia Satie easily allowed himself to indulge in vaguely pornographic jokes. Did he not later describe *Relâche* — the fruit of their collaboration — as a 'ballet obscène'? While nevertheless asserting that he would never wish 'to make a lobster blush, or even an egg'. . .

Erik Satie to Francis Picabia

Arcueil-Cachan, 3 January 1921

Cher Ami — all my cordial good wishes — Cordial-Médoc.

I have one *pensée* for your magazine: 'I would like to play around a really bulging piano'.

Erik Satie

P.S. That seems to me very proper and very artistic without seeming to be. Bien à vous.

Erik Satie

Arcueil-Cachan, 30 Jan. 1921

Mon cher Ami — Did you receive a little *pensée*: 'I would like to play around a really bulging piano'?

Here's another, just as neat: 'It isn't good manners to talk about the cock-up of a question'. . .*

I'd be very pleased if you liked these two 'things' enough to print them in your estimable periodical.

It's vanity, I know; so I beg you to forgive me for this wish.

Amicalement vôtre:

Erik Satie

J'aimerais jouer avec un piano qui aurait une grosse queue.
ERIK SATIE
Ce n'est pas beau de parler du nœud de la question.....
ERIK SATIE

LE PILHAOU-THIBAOU
SUPPLÉMENT ILLUSTRÉ DE "391"

Satie's two '*pensées*' appeared in the *Pilhaou-Thibaou*, an illustrated supplement to *391*, at the very moment when Satie had inscribed his name in the history of Dada, once more without the knowledge of the official claimants to the title. On 24 May 1921, at the Théâtre Michel, Pierre Bertin staged the 'comédie lyrique' *Le Piége de Méduse*, which Satie had written in 1913, that is to say three years before the manifestations at the Cabaret Voltaire and eleven years before publication of the Surrealist Manifesto, but which was nevertheless to figure in the anthologies of Dada and Surrealist theatre compiled later.

Without the least suspicion of this, the Dadaists of *Littérature* accorded the composer the poor average of 2.72 out of 20 in the parlour game they amused themselves with playing in the columns of their magazine: giving marks from −25 to +20 to the leading personalities of past and present. A few lines higher up in the same (alphabetical) role of honour came the wife-murderer Désiré Landru with an only slightly lower average of 2.27.

The most indulgent towards Satie proved to be Aragon and Drieu La Rochelle with +12, the most negative Paul Eluard with −25. Ribemont-Dessaignes gave him +11, Gabrielle Buffet +10, Philippe Soupault +7, Tristan Tzara +3, Benjamin Péret +1, Théodore Fraenkel +4, Jacques Rigaut and André Breton 0. Picabia does not

* The two '*pensées*' by Satie are in fact crude puns that cannot be reproduced in English. Literally, a '*piano avec une grosse queue*' is a piano 'with a big tail' (grand piano is named in French 'piano à queue') and '*le noeud de la question*' is 'the crux of the matter', but '*queue*' and '*noeud*' have also a sexual meaning in slang. [Trsl]

figure among these 'schoolmasters' because he had withdrawn from the movement which, on account of its conspiracies and tribunals, was beginning, he said, to 'suffocate' him.

In June and July 1921, one after the other, Marcel Duchamp and Man Ray arrived from New York. Neither of them had taken part in the Paris quarrels. Man Ray invited representatives of the two camps, without exception, to an exhibition of his paintings on 3 December at the Galerie Six. The new recruit's letter of introduction was signed by Aragon, Arp, Eluard, Max Ernst, Ribemont-Dessaignes, Soupault and Tzara. A marginal note requested visitors not to 'bring flowers, wreaths or umbrellas'. Nevertheless, at the opening it was a gentleman with an umbrella who came to the aid of the artist. Lost in the middle of the crowd and not knowing a word of French, Man Ray has recorded this encounter in his memoirs.

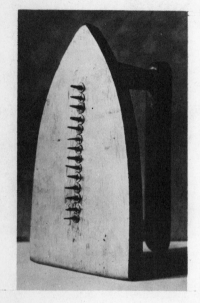

A strange voluble little man in his fifties came over to me and led me to one of my paintings. Strange, because he seemed out of place in this gathering of younger men. With a little white beard, an old-fashioned pince-nez, black bowler hat, black overcoat and umbrella, he looked like an undertaker or an employee of some conservative bank. I was tired with the preparations of the opening, the gallery had no heat, I shivered and said in English that I was cold. He replied in English, took my arm, and led me out of the gallery to a corner café, where he ordered hot grogs. Introducing himself as Erik Satie, he relapsed into French, which I informed him I did not understand. With a twinkle in his eyes he said it did not matter. We had a couple of additional grogs; I began to feel warm and light-headed. Leaving the café, we passed a shop where various household utensils were spread out in front. I picked up a flat-iron, the kind used on coal stoves, asked Satie to come inside with me, where, with his help, I acquired a box of tacks and a tube of glue. Back at the gallery I glued a row of tacks to the smooth surface of the iron, titled it, *The Gift*, and added it to the exhibition. This was my first Dada object in France.

Man Ray and Satie met regularly after this, particularly on Thursdays, when they ate lobster together at a restaurant in the avenue du Maine. Man Ray took several photos of Satie and, later, designed pictures and objects inspired by *Morceaux en forme de poire*. When he was too ill to go home to Arcueil every evening, Satie took a room at the Hôtel Istria in Montparnasse to be near Man Ray, Duchamp and Picabia, who all lived at the same address.

Thanks to the extraordinary impetus lent by Tzara, in a few months the Paris *avant-garde* captured the chief strategic points of the capital. The use of the word '*avant-garde*', which Baudelaire considered inappropriate for an artist because it was borrowed from military vocabulary, thus acquired a real justification. Certain leading figures in the movement then judged that the moment had come to free themselves from the label Dada, which was not of their making and which, moreover, aroused the distrust of those powerful groups whose support was still indispensable. Had not the *Nouvelle Revue Française*, through the pen of André Gide, warned the young editors of *Littérature* against 'these foreigners who pay little heed to our French culture'?

The only means of distinguishing themselves from Dada, for those who had been fellow-travellers up to now, was to prove that it was just one movement among others. To achieve this end Breton had the idea of announcing a 'Congress for the Determination of the Directives and Defence of the Modern Spirit', which later came to be referred to under the abbreviated title of the Congress of Paris. On the organizing committee of this congress he gathered together Amédée Ozenfant, Roger Vitrac, Robert Delaunay, Fernand Léger, Georges Auric and also Jean Paulhan, who was the secretary of the *Nouvelle Revue*

Française. He invited Tristan Tzara to join, but the latter, who no doubt smelled a trap, politely refused, thereby frustrating the whole enterprise. In order to regain the initiative, Breton felt that he now had no other choice than a frontal attack. So on 7 February he published in *Comoedia* a communiqué in which he put readers 'on guard against the activities of an individual known as the promoter of a movement originating in Zurich, which there is no point in defining more clearly and which today no longer has any real existence'.

Since the form and the spirit of this communiqué were so poorly conceived, Tzara had no difficulty in finding at La Rotonde a few good friends who would join him in signing a rejoinder. The following day *Comoedia* carried the following open letter.

Paris, 13 February 1922

Dear Sir,

The bureaucratic and ridiculous preparations for the great Congress to fix the limits of modern art, and the cheap commercial publicity attached to it, are already bearing fruit and leading to complications in which the true spirit of the organizers becomes apparent: the wish to destroy everything that is living, and reactionary zeal in every domain. They go so far as to reproach a person with having come from Zurich. Quite apart from any personal concern, we believe it is time to put a stop to these popish goings on and to defend our freedom. We wish to consult you on this subject and request you to come to the Closerie des Lilas on 17 February.

Paul Eluard, G. Ribemont-Dessaignes
Erik Satie, Tristan Tzara

Seeing Tzara less isolated than he had supposed, Breton looked around for other supporters, beginning with Picabia, whose break with Dada was fresh in everyone's memory. It must be noted that the Dadaism to which Picabia objected was precisely the Dadaism of the pontiffs and conspirators embodied by Breton. In any case, Breton could not be bothered with such details at this moment, when he would have paid a high price for any support, including that of Cocteau, someone he had despised up till then and conscientiously resumed despising as soon as this parenthesis was closed.

André Breton to Francis Picabia

Paris, 15 February 1922

Très cher Ami [. . .] For some days Tzara has been expending unparalleled energy in wriggling and writhing in the spot in which the Congress's letter has put him. [. . .] He is organizing a meeting against the Congress on Friday evening at the Closerie des Lilas. The invitation to this meeting is signed by Satie, Ribemont-Dessaignes, Paul Eluard and Tzara. [. . .] Eluard has declared that, although I may be right, there are greater advantages to be derived today from supporting Tzara. As for Ribemont-Dessaignes, you know what he has against me. Satie's case seems more obscure to me, in view of the attitudes of Cocteau and Auric, the latter being perfectly clear, the former being less favourable to Tzara than to us [. . .] Let's wait and see [. . .]

Je suis très affectueusement à vous

André Breton

Francis Picabia to André Breton

Saint-Raphaël, 17 February 1922

Mon cher Breton [. . .] I'm glad we are friends [. . .] Ribemont-Dessaignes is a fool. [. . .] Satie's case is extraordinary, it must come from his great 'friendship' for Auric and above all Cocteau. Satie is a man you can't trifle with! He's a crafty and wily old artist — at least, that's what he thinks of himself. Personally, I think just the opposite! He's a very sensitive man, proud, a real sad child whom alcohol occasionally renders optimistic — He's a good friend whom I love dearly. Tzara must want to make use of him like a flag (a white flag). Satie will be glad to come over to us again [. . .] Shake all the *friendly* hands around you, mon cher Breton. Très affectueusement vôtre

Francis Picabia

On 17 February everyone (except Picabia who, as usual, was hibernating on the Riviera) came together at the Closerie des Lilas. Under the chairmanship of a hilarious Satie — a witness, Matthew Josephson, tells us — an improvised tribunal condemned Breton and his project for a Congress of Paris without appeal. Satie took malicious pleasure in drafting a press release 'in the pompous style affected by Breton'.

For over a year, there were no more *avant-garde* demonstrations in Paris. At the end of spring 1923 Tzara, who could bear it no longer, decided to organize a so-called Soirée du Coeur à Barbe in memory of a publication of the same name which he had brought out at the time of the Congress of Paris affair. He called upon Satie to take care of the musical section.

Erik Satie to Tristan Tzara

Friday 29 June 1923

Cher Ami — I'm frightfully sorry: It's much too late to reach an agreement with musicians. I spent all day yesterday trying to find someone. What can we do. . .???

Give up the musical section — which, anyhow, is of only limited interest.

The time of year — *fin de saison* — compels us to abandon many projects. I think it would be sensible to do the same thing with the musical project. Yes.

Votre vieil ami:

ES

P.S. Put it off until everybody is back in September, cher Ami.

Tzara was not a man to be stopped by a few difficulties and so the Soirée du Coeur à Barbe took place. Accompanied by Marcelle Meyer, the wife of Pierre Bertin, Satie played his *Morceaux en forme de poire*, chosen no doubt on account of the provocative — and hence potentially Dadaist — nature of its title. Some of Tzara's former adversaries came, this time to support him. Others, however, demonstrated in a manner Tzara had

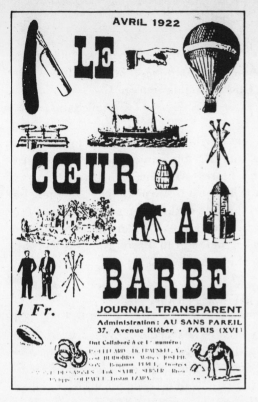

certainly not wished for. The following is an extract from the account of this memorable evening published by Roger Vitrac in *Les Hommes du Jour*:

> Pierre de Massot received a blow from Breton's walking-stick, Jacques Baron was slapped in the face by Breton, Crevel was roughed up by Eluard, Gilbert Charles by Max Morise. M. Fees fought with Marcel Arland. Breton, Péret and Desnos were forcibly ejected by the police amid shouts of 'Murderer! Get out!'

After a night's reflection, however, Tzara was ready for a general reconciliation. This time he could not persuade Satie to go along with him.

Erik Satie to Tristan Tzara

Arcueil, 7 July 1923

Cher Ami — Impossible this evening. You must realize that that's out of the question even for a minute.

I like you a lot . . . but I don't like Breton and the others . . . So? . . . Not this evening: another time, if you like.

Bien à vous, Cher Ami. Bon courage

Erik Satie

The following year, on the occasion of the première of *Mercure*, Aragon and Breton came and demonstrated against Satie under pressure, this time, from Georges Auric, whom Satie had just disowned. Since, by then, he was no longer on the side of the former organizers of the Congress of Paris, Picabia — still on holiday on the Riviera — received news from Paris from his faithful 'dogsbody' Pierre de Massot.

Pierre de Massot to Francis Picabia

16 June 1924

[. . .] On Sunday evening a scandal provoked by Aragon who, pursued by the cops, broke away from them and jumped onto the stage yelling: 'Bravo Picasso, down with Satie'. At the back, Breton and his companions were yelling with Darius Milhaud. I roared: 'Bravo Satie'. The performance was broken off. The police got them out in spite of the courage of Aragon (it must be said), who kept shouting: 'Nom de Dieu, down with the cops'. I must tell you that Auric had been plotting with Aragon and Breton long before the performance [. . .]

P. de M.

Fifty years later, while confusing the Rose + Croix with the Freemasons and limiting Erik Satie's work to popular songs, Aragon made this declaration, which shows that the motives behind this attack had nothing to do with music: 'Breton hated all music. Not me. And especially the comic songs of Satie, whom I knew and who was a' Freemason before he joined the Communist Party.'

As for Breton, in 1955 he wrote: 'Satie liked to say that the piano, like money, is only pleasant to him who touches it: that puts me at ease, I who have from birth had a quarrel with instrumental music. I regret all the more not having understood until too late, after his death, the exceptional being that he was and that a curtain of thorns — his malice, his studied mannerisms — had hidden from me.'

After *Mercure* Breton and his friends took the precaution of singling out Picasso, with whom they didn't wish to quarrel, from 'those around him'. So they published in the Press a vibrant 'Homage to Picasso', no doubt in the hope of stirring up friction between the painter and the composer. At this time Satie was contributing to *les feuilles libres*. Wieland Mayr, the editor-in-chief of this literary review, who had written to ask him if there was any truth in all these stories, received the following reply:

Erik Satie to Wieland Mayr

Saturday, 21 June 1924

Cher Monsieur Mayr — Herewith a theatre ticket (free, of course).

Mercure will only be performed next week (Thursday 26, Friday 27 , Saturday 28). Yes. . .

It was kind of you to write. Believe me, there is no divergence of views between Picasso and me. It's all a 'gimmick' by my old friend, the famous writer Bretuchon (*who came to create a disturbance and attract attention by his shabby appearance and deplorable rudeness*). Yes . . . Let us pray the Lord to inspire in him pious thoughts and to receive him at his Holy Table. . . As for me, I don't give a damn. . . And how!. . .

Perhaps he'll go to hell?. . . We'll never know. Yes. [. . .]

Bonjour, cher Monsieur Mayr. Amicalement vôtre:

Erik Satie

The day after the evening on which 'the famous writer Bretuchon' had come to boo him along with his friends, Satie had written to Milhaud to reassure him. He related: 'As I came out I passed the *pseudo-dadas*. They didn't say a word to me'.

Francis Picabia

RELÂCHE

Two days before causing the row at the Soirée de Paris, Breton had disdainfully declined an invitation from Picabia to contribute to *391*, along with Duchamp, Man Ray, Pierre de Massot, Robert Desnos and Erik Satie. 'May Satie's old grimaces,' he concluded his reply, 'compensate you for our refusal'.

Picabia's only response was to print Breton's letter in his magazine with the commentary: 'After I've smoked cigarettes it's not my habit to keep the butts.'

Apart from his weariness with the quarrels in Paris, Picabia's attitude is to be explained by the fact that at this very moment he was collaborating closely with Satie on his first undertaking for the stage, an adventure by which he was particularly thrilled. The call had come from Satie, but Picabia had managed to gain the dominant position in the enterprise, instead of the incidental one that had been offered him. This is how it happened:

After the success of *La Création du Monde* — libretto by Cendrars, music by Milhaud, design by Léger — Rolf de Maré, director of the Ballets Suédois, had asked Cendrars to present him with a new project, this time using the music of Erik Satie.

Erik Satie to Rolf de Maré

Friday 23 November 1923

Mon cher Directeur — A thousand thanks. I received the cheque. Yes.

How are you?

Herewith the contract which I've signed.

We are working on the ballet, Cendrars & I. It will be a Parisian work — from Paris. I shall be very happy to collaborate on your future productions. Personally, I'm very fond of you; & I'm convinced that with Jean Börlin & you, we shall, Cendrars & I, do good work.

Amicalement vôtre:

Erik Satie

Shortly afterwards a 'big motor-fuel deal' called Blaise Cendrars to Rio de Janeiro. During the voyage on board the Formose, Cendrars did not forget to be a poet. One of the poems in blank verse which he wrote at that time, *Bagage*, draws up an inventory of his suitcase. Among other things listed we find: 'the manuscript of a ballet for the next season of the Ballets Suédois which I wrote on board between Le Havre and La Pallice from which place I sent it to Satie.'

In his manuscript, Cendrars had noted the names of three painters who might be entrusted with the scenery for such a piece: the cartoonist Gus Bofa, the Brazilian woman painter Tarsila do Amaral, and Francis Picabia. Satie settled in favour of the last, who also seemed to him the one most capable of counterbalancing Jean Cocteau — now become his bête noire — on his favourite ground, Parisianism.

Picabia being, once more, on the Côte d'Azur, Satie gave their mutual friend Pierre de Massot the job of communicating to him his proposal.

Pierre de Massot to Francis Picabia

Tuesday 22 January 1924

Mon cher Picabia,

I'm writing to you immediately to let you know about a rather important business which, apart from the Fr 10,000 it is bound to bring you, will arouse enormous interest, amazement, and throw a bomb from the extreme Right to the extreme Left. I would never permit myself to advise you; however, I cannot conceal the fact that I should be heartbroken if you refused. I am commissioned by ERIK SATIE to ask for your collaboration in a ballet for the Suédois: *you will have complete freedom. Everything is expected of you.* Hébertot and de Maré would be delighted. For the first time, the Théâtre des Champs Elysées will perhaps make a real revolution that has nothing in common with the *Mariés* [*de la Tour Eiffel* by Cocteau] demonstration. Perhaps a new DADA.

Think about it and say yes.

Above all, don't imagine that I am an interested party. I'm doing this *out of affection and admiration* for you. The scenario is not by me, it's by Cendrars.

Reply as soon as possible. Croyez à l'amitié fidèle de

P. de M.

Pierre de Massot to Francis Picabia

26 January 1924

My dear Picabia,

I found your long letter yesterday [. . .] As to the ballet, you can go ahead: you have *complete freedom.* The public (from which the 'friends' will be shut out) must shout: it will be the great event. The scenario is elastic. The title *Après Dîner!* A drunken gentleman comes out of a restaurant and wonders what to do: it's up to you to imagine the enchantments of his 'Parisian' night. Here you are in the period you yourself announced: the silk-stocking period.

I have no more advice to give you, but on this occasion you can do whatever you like. I can't write any more either since I've been drinking, dancing and making love [. . .]

Massot

PIERRE DE MASSOT ET SON AUTRUCHE

FRANCIS PICABIA
23 avril 1924

Francis Picabia

Pierre de Massot to Francis Picabia

3 February 1924

Mon cher Picabia,

I have seen Satie who was delighted with your yes; you will benefit from a marvellous collaboration and an unheard of freedom.

Here is Cendrars' scenario, which is in no way final and on which you can embroider to your heart's delight, on condition that you leave the same time-period, the same duration (indispensable for the music and the work of the composer).

Already the Cocteau crowd has got wind of it. Don't turn down the opportunity to dynamite Paris (this is your chance) [. . .]

Massot

Erik Satie to Francis Picabia

Friday 8 February 1924

Cher Ami — A thousand thanks — I think your 'little thing' will not be bad at all. Yes. .

For my part, I want to be very 'Parisian' — That'll be 'chic!' — very 'chic' . . .

Come back soon, won't you? I can't really work until you're back near us.

Bon souvenir à votre chère compagne & à vous même.

ES

When years later he proposed the libretto *Après Dîner* to another musician, the Danish composer Knudage Riisager, Cendrars changed one detail, which though in itself of little importance, is not without piquancy. The sign over the bar where the 'drunken gentleman' and his friends were presumed to finish their evening was, in the first version, *Chez Francis*, which was none other than the name of the large café opposite the Théâtre des Champs Elysées, the home ground of the Ballets Suédois. In the new manuscript this sign was replaced by *Chez Blaise*. This change was, rather childishly, an act of revenge because in the final libretto it was 'Francis' Picabia who had replaced 'Blaise' Cendrars. In fact, while Cendrars was still hanging around in Brazil, Picabia took the opportunity to discard the role of mere scene painter that had been given him. Somewhat forgetting his friend Blaise, Satie was overjoyed, for his part, to be able to push ahead with his work with the possibility of discussing the undertaking with someone on the spot. Picabia lost no time returning to Paris, which Satie never left, except for one very short trip to Brussels. It was from there, after delivering a lecture on the *Esprit musical*, organized by La Lanterne Sourde at the Salle Delgay, that he communicated his satisfaction to the go-between.

Erik Satie to Pierre de Massot

Brussels, 18 March 1924

Cher Ami — I'm coming back to Paris on Monday evening (next Monday).

Thanks for your note.

'Très chic' Picabia's scenario.

Mille choses à la charmante Miss, je vous prie, & à vous-même

ES

Erik Satie to Rolf de Maré

Wednesday 2 April 1924

Mon cher Directeur & Ami — I've been told you're back. Great! Yes. . . I'd like to see you on the subject of the ballet. There's something new — new — which seems to be extremely interesting, very interesting indeed. . .

When could I see you? I'm entirely at your disposal.

My address? Erik Satie, Arcueil-Cachan.

My very good wishes to Börlin, please. Bien à vous je suis

Erik Satie

The 'something new' was precisely Picabia's scenario, which, in fact, was nothing but a rewrite — simplified and, no doubt, more gripping — of Cendrars' text. On his return Cendrars never stopped crying thief, while Picabia prudently back-tracked. In any case, it was too late. Germaine Everling, Picabia's companion at that time, has left an account of the events:

Francis Picabia

The evening the contract was signed with de Maré, Satie, as usual, drank enough small glasses of quetsch to fill a magnum bottle if they had all been added together. Full of enthusiasm, he kept repeating: 'Ah, mon vieux! C'est chic! Ça va être épatant!' And from that moment he came to the Tremblay every Sunday; he was full of good humour and confidence, wittily teasing any of his contemporaries against whom he had some complaint. He appreciated the understanding he met with from Picabia and the close collaboration in which their work developed. The construction of his music evolved in constant keeping with the painter's thought. Picabia worked equally joyfully. He wanted a title that would symbolize a sort of schism between what had been done up till then and what he dreamed of doing: that was why he chose *Relâche*.

'Relâche' has two meanings in French: relaxation, respite, and 'no performance'.

Satie approved the choice: 'In this way', he remarked, 'we are certain to have the title upon at least one Paris theatre every evening and, some evenings, on all the theatres at the same time!'

The major part of the work was completed in the course of the autumn. Satie's friends were kept informed as the various stages were reached, as well as of his successive states of mind. Greatly tormented at this time by his differences with Auric, Poulenc and Cocteau, Satie even ceased contributing to *les feuilles libres* — one of his few sources of remuneration — when he realized that he would not be able to write everything that was on his mind.

Erik Satie to Pierre de Massot

Sunday 27 July. Yes. Mon cher Ami — Thank you for your kind note. When are you coming back?

I'm working on *Relâche* as much as I can. In any case, I've done the first part (*half, therefore*). Yes . . . I'm quite pleased.

Note that I've done all the music myself. All the flats (*above all*), all the sharps (*even the daggers*) have been done entirely (*from head to foot!*) by me.

All this is very odd, & indicates great strength of character (frank and loyal). So I bless myself. . . Yes.

Amicalement vôtre:

Erik Satie

Erik Satie to Darius Milhaud

Sunday 10 August 1924

Cher Grand Ami — You must have noticed that our two notes crossed. A curious case of telepathy.

Herewith the 'little thing' presented differently. . . Auric won't like it: 'Ugh!' he'll say.

I'm working hard. It's going fine. I'm not displeased. . . A lot of '*tears in the eyes*'. The attached example will tell you much about that.

Is your mother well? Remember me to her and to your father, please.

And the 'gentille petite Dame'? You mustn't forget to give my kindest regards to her (play her a bit of the following little tune).

Amicalement vôtre:

Erik Satie

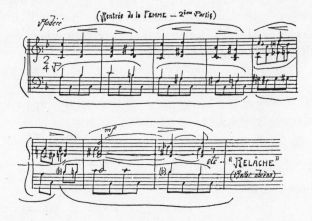

Erik Satie to Germaine Everling

Wednesday 27 August 1924

Chère Madame — Thank you for your charming letter. Yes . . . *Relâche* (the finale) is being copied out. So the ballet is entirely composed. I'm working on the orchestration. . . Yes. . .

De Maré will be coming back at the beginning of September. Börlin must have finished the choreographic study of the first part, the part I sent him in Nice. Yes. . .

How is your health? Good, j'espère (de famille)*. Yes. . . Let Picabia take care of himself. Yes. . . I'm as bored as in an oven. Yes. . . I'm going up in smoke with anger (French tobacco). . . Yes. . . Life is too much like Death — like Death-Bach (a 'Hun' swearword). . . .

Amitiés amicales d'ami à vous deux

ES

Erik Satie to Paul Collaer

Saturday 18 October 1924

Cher adorable Ami — forgive me for not having replied sooner to your charming letter. . . You can imagine I've been working, and how! In two days the orchestration of *Relâche* will be finished. . . What a ballet!

The première will be lively, believe me. The enemy forces — *this time* — will meet ours. We are mobilizing!. . .

I've been suffering horribly, mon cher Ami: apart from rheumatic pains, I've had neuritis!

Bien vôtre: ES

Erik Satie to Marcel Raval
editor of *les feuilles libres*

Tuesday 21 Oct. 1924, Arcueil, Seine

Mon cher Directeur & Ami — I have just received your card & thank you for it. What a thing telepathy is!. . . Yes: I was picking up my pen to write to you about . . . rather delicate subjects that demand clarification.

* An untranslatable pun: *j'espère* = 'I hope' and *pére de famille* = 'father of the family' [Trsl]

It is all the easier for me to speak to you about . . . these things because you are in no way involved (*or very indirectly*).

You know the '*politico-musical*' position of the Group of '*Six*': concessions, short-changed alliances (*Laloy, Marnold, Roland Manuel*). All of this directed against me.

Unfortunately for my opponents, if they are short-changing, I, for my part, am not too short-sighted and I've seen their 'tricks' before they even set them in motion. The 'arrangements' don't bother me at all, as you can imagine. It was impossible not to draw attention to them publicly: otherwise I should have appeared to approve of them. . . At least a little. . . I don't like it. . . Yes. . .

While working on my article for your delightful review, I felt that I could not act freely & that your personal attachments to some of the '*Six*' limited my field of action, and that at a moment when the struggle was growing more intense. . . . In your charming card you speak to me of '*Relâche*'. It's '*Relâche*' that will give the signal for 'departure'. With '*Relâche*' we are entering into a new period. I say this immodestly, but I say it. . . Picabia is cracking the egg, & we shall set out 'forward', leaving the Cocteaus and other 'blinkered' people behind us,. . .

Do you see why I can't write my article?. . . . It would be impossible for you to publish it. If you went ahead with it, you would have to break with friends (*who are no longer mine, fortunately*). . . Am I not right?. . . Long live Freedom (*so rare*)!. . . Yes. . .

I'm writing to friend Mayr to tell him the 'Thing'.

Don't bear me a grudge, Cher Directeur & Ami: don't imagine I've forgotten how kind you have always been to me.

Amicalement vôtre:

Erik Satie

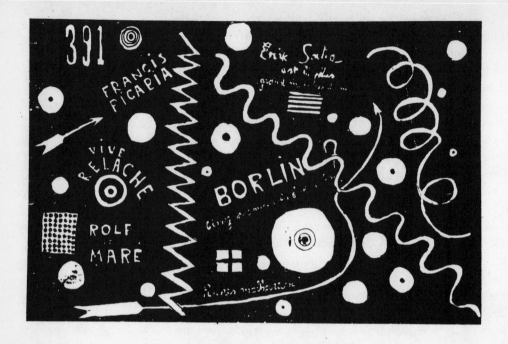

At the time of *La Diva de 'L'Empire'*, the cinema was regarded as a fairground attraction. Thus in the music hall of 1900 a short film — preferably comic — was often shown between the two parts of a revue. A passionate lover of the cinema (he had been assistant and interpreter to Abel Gance), Cendrars may have had the idea of reverting to this old custom for Satie's ballet. Picabia also thought this a splendid idea, all the more so since he saw in it an opportunity to bring about the first meeting between the cinema and Dada.

The Théâtre des Champs Elysées published a review, *Théâtre et Comoedia illustré*, accompanied by a cinematographic supplement edited by a certain René Chomette. Under the pseudonym of René Clair he had just shot a highly imaginative feature film, *Paris qui dort*. It was therefore quite natural that the 'cinema' of *Relâche* should be entrusted to him.

On the basis of a scenario sketched out by Picabia on a sheet of paper bearing the letterhead of Maxim's, the smart restaurant of la Madeleine, where Rolf de Maré often invited him to dinner, René Clair produced in one week a short which he described as 'a child's dream.' As actors he had used the authors of the ballet themselves, Satie and Picabia, the director and the choreographer of the Ballets Suédois, Rolf de Maré and Jean Börlin, followed by their friends, Marcel Achard, Georges Charensol, Man Ray and Marcel Duchamp. A portrait of Duchamp appeared during these same days on the cover of *391* no. 19, superimposed on the manifesto of Instantaneism, a movement that was not, in fact, destined to endure more than an 'instant' — precisely for the length of time it took to produce *Relâche*, an 'instantaneist ballet' — and which had doubtless only been launched in order to rally Breton, who had just published his Surrealist Manifesto.

Before composing the music for the 'cinema' of *Relâche*, Satie had demanded to know the exact timing of every sequence.

Erik Satie to René Clair

Thursday 23 Oct. 1924

Cher Monsieur Clair — How about the film?. . . When?. . . Time is passing (and will not pass again). I fear you may have forgotten me. Yes.

Send me quickly the details of your work which is so marvellous. Thanks a lot.

Bien vôtre je suis: ES

The first film music composed 'frame by frame' thus saw the light, at a time when the cinema was still silent.

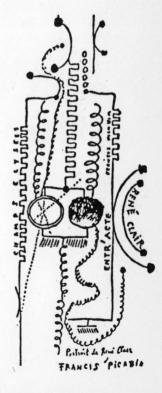

Relâche and its cinematographic interlude — entitled
Entr'acte — were presented on 4 December. Fernand
Léger wrote that this 'instantaneist ballet' represented
'many kicks up many backsides, sacred or not'. Other
critics, such as Georges Auric, by contrast, dismissed this
work as totally worthless. Roland Manuel went so far as to
head his vilification *Adieu Satie*.

DEPARTURE

The moment to say 'adieu' had, in fact, arrived. While he was working on *Relâche* Satie informed his friends, here and there, of certain complaints from which he was beginning to suffer. At the end of 1924 when he invited Roger Désormière, who had directed *Mercure* and was to direct *Relâche*, to dinner, he told him that henceforth he would only be eating 'vegetables'. Unfortunately it was too late to counteract the cirrhosis of the liver that he had been contributing to throughout his lifetime.

The disease is pretty common among natives of Calvados, who are constantly tempted by the liquor of their native soil. In Satie's case, this predisposition had doubtless been aggravated by the constantly difficult circumstances of his life, the consequences of his intransigence. Often reduced to dependence on his friends' generosity, he noted with humour: 'It's odd. You find people in every bar willing to offer you a drink. No one ever dreams of presenting you with a sandwich.'

To celebrate the authors of *Relâche*, Rolf de Maré had arranged a sumptuous midnight supper at the Boeuf sur le Toit on New Year's Eve. Satie was ill and unable to attend.

Erik Satie to Rolf de Maré

Arcueil, 10 January 1924 (25, I mean)

Mon cher Directeur,

Forgive me for not having thanked you earlier for your kind invitation of 31 December.

I was too tired and in too much pain to take advantage of it.

I should so much have liked to see you that evening to give you in person my New Year greetings and my best wishes for a good journey. . . I should also have told you what a charming Director you have been to me.

Bonjour, mon cher Directeur, mille choses to Börlin, please. Croyez-moi vôtre tout dévoué

Erik Satie

Darius Milhaud reports that from this moment on Satie made a habit of coming to Paris every day, lunching in turn at the homes of Derain, Braque or Milhaud himself:

He ate very little and sat close to the fireplace with his overcoat on, his hat pulled down to his eyes and clutching his umbrella; he remained like this, motionless and silent, until the time came for him to catch his train back to Arcueil. We didn't like these constant journeys back and forth and finally managed to persuade him to move to Paris. He wanted to go to the Hôtel Istria in Montparnasse; he was promised a room at a later date. In the meantime, thanks to the intervention of Jean Wiéner, whose father had been manager of the Grand Hôtel, a place was found for him there. Still with his hat, his coat and his umbrella, he spent his days sitting in a large easy-chair looking at himself in the mirror facing him and opening and closing the lock on the door by means of a complicated system of strings that he had devised himself.

He was so exasperated by the telephone that we avoided calling him, but we often went to see him. His room was comfortable and quiet, but Satie didn't want to stay there and, in spite of the noisy proximity of painters and students, he moved to the Hôtel Istria as soon as he could get a room there. When the doctor ordered his transfer to the hospital, the Count de Beaumont, who had established a ward in the Hôpital Saint-Joseph, supported our application and obtained a private room for him. Satie asked Madeleine [Milhaud] to pack his bag; as she knew him to be capable of inexplicable rages if things were not put exactly where he wanted them, she asked Braque to stand between them so that Satie could not see how she was packing his bag; we all went with our friend in the ambulance [. . .] During the drive, Satie joked: 'Come on, let's have a drink!' as we passed the café where he had composed some of his most beautiful pages [. . .] At the hospital, the nun who laid out his personal possessions could quickly see that she was dealing with no ordinary patient. The only toiletry articles Satie possessed were a horsehair brush and a pummice stone with which no doubt he rubbed his skin.

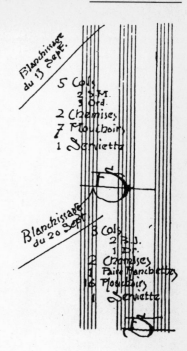

His friends took turns at his bedside. Henri Sauguet recalls: 'One day he asked me to lay out the many gifts his friends had brought him, which he did not wish to touch, leaving them intact in their wrappings (I have been told that on his deathbed Braque did likewise)'. Jacques Maritain, who had been brought by Pierre de Massot, suggested to Satie that he should bring the Abbé Saint to see him. 'Fine,' Satie replied, 'I'd like to see a saint before I die.' He asked this priest if his visit was due to the fact that he played in a band and told his friends afterwards that he looked like a 'Modigliani on a blue background'. Maritain later insisted on the spontaneity of what Satie himself called his 'sort of conversion': 'On Good Friday he had confessed, and as he had forgotten his prayers he asked the nun who was looking after him to help him to do penance. Together they recited the Lord's prayer and the Hail Mary. Satie shed tears.'

Robert Caby

Little by little visits grew less frequent, everyone's time being taken up by their own obligations.

Pierre de Massot to Francis Picabia

19 June 1925

[. . .] I haven't had time to go and see Satie for quite a while [. . .]

Massot

All of a sudden his condition worsened. Exposure of his bare chest to the icy air of a winter's night, which had enabled him to escape from military service forty years before, had no doubt rendered him more fragile. An attack of pleurisy now affected his already greatly weakened constitution. Léopold Survage relates: 'One day I went to see him with Picasso and we straightened his sweat-soaked sheets. He had become extremely gentle with everyone.'

One fine morning, having decided to quit the stage, Caryathis started burning her posters and costumes on a brazier in the middle of her garden. The fire had just started on her costume for *La Belle Excentrique* when she was brought a telegram from Georges Auric, announcing that Satie was in a very bad way:

> I hurried to see him and found him at death's door, but still alive. A ferocious will to live could be read in his expression of rage, while his body was no more than a shadow. A bell tinkled outside, followed by a hurried footstep. Satie sat up and said to me: 'That one's beaten me to it.'

Claire Goll saw him struggling on his death bed, yelling: 'The letter . . . where's the letter?' 'He threw back the covers and knocked over his medicine bottles in order to get his hands on this mysterious correspondence. That was his last turn of the key, forever locking up all communication.'

And yet, on one of his very last days, he greeted young Max Fontaine, a friend of recent date, with an amused expression and whispered in his ear, so as not to be overheard by the nuns: 'Last night I dreamed I had two willies! You can't imagine how many things you can do with that thingamajig!'

On 2 July Madeleine Milhaud, back from her honeymoon with Darius, found Satie's bed empty. Accompanied by Désormière, Valentine Hugo went to the chapel where his body had been lying since the previous evening and was struck by the regularity of his features, normally obscured by his pince-nez.

The majority of his friends, away on holiday, were informed by the newspapers. Thus Pierre de Massot:

When the news reached me through *Comoedia* I had just come back from a fishing trip on the lake of Aix-les-Bains. I opened the magazine: a photograph, a brief obituary notice. Everything had changed as though night had suddenly fallen and wrapped this smiling, sunny countryside in darkness.

Poulenc, too, was far from Paris. Before leaving he had asked in vain for permission to visit the 'Bon Maître' in hospital. 'No, no, I'd rather not see them,' Satie had replied. 'I prefer to stick with their *adieu*. One must be intransigent to the very end.' A childhood friend of Poulenc's, Raymonde Linossier, undertook to keep him informed of events. A lawyer by training, she was attached to the Musée Guimet as a specialist in Oriental art and was the author of a small book, *Bibi la Bibiste*, admired by Ezra Pound. She had met Satie at Adrienne Monnier's Maison des Amis des Livres.

Raymonde Linossier to Francis Poulenc

Monday 6 [July 1925]

Cher enfant,

I'm sorry not to have given you details about poor Satie earlier. He was buried this morning at Arcueil, in a countrified cemetery where a coffin of pinewood painted red to imitate mahogany was placed directly in the ground.

I saw the poor old fellow on Wednesday, the morning of his death. I went into his room and found him asleep. His face was very much changed since my last visit, partly by over-deep sleep, and covered with flies that didn't even wake him. Naturally I didn't want to wake him, so I left. Then I had a chat with the nun who was looking after him, who told me of the profound change that had occurred during these last few days. She was expecting the end without suspecting just how near it was. It seems he slept all day and died in the evening, I believe without regaining consciousness. Next day Madeleine Milhaud found his room empty.

For a few days he had taken no nourishment whatever, except for champagne and elixir of paregoric. Now that he's dead, I'll tell you about the frightful visit that upset me so. Without having been warned, I found myself confronted by a man who no longer had his wits about him and who rambled for two hours. This decline of the Bon Maître of times past was terrible to see.

He had been very pleased to see me — and talked only of me to the little monkey when she came back to Paris. He asked for me and his sleep prevented me from seeing him again.

His brother learned of his death from his neighbour's concierge, who asked him if he knew the Monsieur Satie the newspapers were talking about. They're making preparations to bury him. When I say 'they', I mean the little monkey, because she's playing the widow. She said: 'His brother and I have decided to have him buried in Arcueil. I'm going to have the seals affixed', etc. . . . Odious under these circumstances as always, this morning she put her earrings in mourning — huge cabochons of black glass.

The burial in Arcueil was fine. No doubt a lot of people were prevented from coming and only the elegant element, unemployed and pederast, was represented. But the setting was pleasant and the good people of Arcueil, café companions and others, followed the cortège. It would have been a pity to see Satie, after his death, taken possession of by the kind of society people he didn't give a damn for. Darius looking impressively downcast. Auric, bowled over, looked like a dog, as he did at the première of *Les Matelots* — he was very close to tears. Cocteau sobbed rather noisily. Valentine was made up as though for a formal occasion. Forgive me, but I couldn't help looking at the ceremony through Satie's eyes.

As for the flowers, I didn't ask Cocteau's advice, first because I didn't understand your telegram on this point, and then because I couldn't see what advice he could have given me.

I was afraid — rightly — that people wouldn't turn up on account of the holidays and the distance to Arcueil. I was also afraid that the funeral might be rather poor and I

wanted the Bon Maître to be treated as a maître and not as a penniless musician. So I sent a very fine wreath on your behalf (salmon-pink roses and hydrangeas of the same colour) and I must say that what other people sent barely covered the catafalque and that your wreath and mine alone decorated the church. There was only a scrap of black cloth behind the altar.

The only flowers sent by official bodies were from the Ballets Suédois, in bad taste like their performances, Rouart & Lerolle, the Amis du Vieil Arcueil and a touching wreath of violets, costing about 25 francs, with a ribbon saying: '*To Monsieur Satie from his fellow tenants.*' He must have been very much loved over there. The woman at the pâtisserie asked me all sorts of details about his death.

As to the questions you put to me — I'm sure extreme unction was administered, since he was at St Joseph's, a religious hospital where he had already taken communion, which authorized the nuns to give him the last rites.

About the manuscripts, I know nothing. His brother arrived on Saturday and no one entered his room after his death. I'll phone Darius tomorrow to get his news and I'll ask him.

There, mon vieux, those are all the details I can give you. I have been very sad to see this man leave us who was always so friendly, and even affectionate towards me. That kind of tenderness which he showed me right up to the last moment and from our very first meeting, seven or eight years ago, touched and — I should even say greatly — flattered me. And there were many reasons why we should have understood each other so well. I was struck by this when I saw some of his Arcueil friends.

Even for me your quarrel with him created, if not a coldness, at least a feeling of uneasiness. Otherwise I would have gone to see him sooner. It's true that if I had gone sooner, he might have thrown me out before his death, as he did with many of his friends.

Forgive me if this letter sounds very disconnected. No sooner was I back from the funeral than I had to give law examinations to young girls who knew nothing — then to discuss business — and go out this evening — it's very late and I have to get up early tomorrow.

And then it was an old friend who has seriously occupied my thoughts for two weeks and it's hard to give up our habit of drinking an aperitif together while speaking ill of people, with his umbrella between the two of us. . .

Tendrement vôtre

Y.F.A.

On the evening of the funeral, Conrad Satie also felt the need to write. Was he thinking of publishing an article? Was he writing for himself? As his brother had sometimes done, he described his impressions, speaking of himself in the third person singular:

> For months Erik Satie had been in a clinic in Montrouge, his body terrifyingly thin and his face of a waxen tinge that left little hope. His mind had preserved its lucidity. Le Bon Maître had a horror of the frequent tapping of the lungs that had to be carried out since his double pneumonia. Cirrhosis of the liver did not prevent him from being given platefuls of cabbage to eat, which he much enjoyed. No doubt he was regarded as past saving.
>
> In the end, he did not touch the bottles of champagne that people brought him, but he m de plans for the following summer.
>
> He died quietly, with no intensification of his daily pains. Arcueil-Cachan, three kilometres from Paris, is a pleasant large village on the outskirts, almost a small town. How many times did he not return there on foot, long after midnight and, he said, not hesitating to stop under a gaslight to jot down a musical idea when it came to him.
>
> He lived in a house on an acute angle, between two streets, which Utrillo could have painted, with a bistro down below where he sometimes copied out his music.
>
> His room had a single window on the second floor.

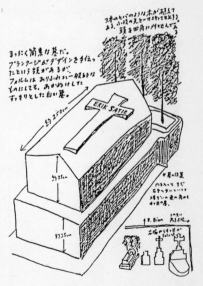

None of even his best friends, to my knowledge, ever entered it. He had created for himself his own seclusion there.

A local resident told me: 'He very nearly became a town councillor.' Many workers were his friends. They had been able to appreciate his mind and also his music long before the snobs and the wealthy people who sweetened the material side of his life towards the end, but among whom he can never have found peace of mind.

Satie used to say: 'I have great confidence in the good Lord; when I'm dead He will do with me absolutely whatever he likes.'

A friend relates that ten months ago he saw him down in one evening ten black coffees with liqueur brandy. I never saw him drink more than three in a row.

His brother is there, robust, correct. He says 'I haven't seen him for a year. After my wife's death I told him I didn't want to see anyone and he granted this wish all too perfectly, since his death took me by surprise.'

The church of Arcueil, not far from the grandiose aqueduct, is old and small. The nave is filled with friends. The priest chants the Mass in a timid voice; perhaps he is afraid of this musical audience. The little choirboy who carried the heavy silver crucifix fidgets and can't sit still. In the side chapel a marriage is taking place at the same time, four people all told whose gestures recall Henri Rousseau.

We file past and throw holy water on the coffin; Jean Cocteau bursts into tears. Among those present, I am told, is one who, in the course of a polemic with Satie in the press last year, derisively sent him a jumping-jack and a rattle as though for someone who has lapsed into childhood. But everything passes. . .

The little funeral procession wends its way through the little town. At the cemetery there are a few men with suntanned faces who refuse the aspergillum containing holy water and merely throw a handful of earth on the coffin.

In the religious hospital where he was, he took the Easter sacrament this year, but it must have been for the first time.

Brancusi's eyes are moist. A few weeks ago he tried to revive Satie by bringing him yoghurt and chicken soup every day that he had made himself at home, and Satie did show some improvement, but it did not last.

Satie and Brancusi used to tease one another unmercifully, untiringly for hours on end, without getting annoyed, throwing jokes like paving stones into one another's face. The spectators would become exhausted. Not they. They were carried along by the purity of their character and their work.

Darius Milhaud is losing a friend who loved him dearly.

We move away from the burial vault. I hear Satie's bantering voice saying to God: 'Just give me time to put on a petticoat, and then I'm yours.'

He was so alive.

LIST OF ILLUSTRATIONS

CHRONOLOGY

1866   17 May, at Honfleur (Calvados), birth of Eric Alfred Leslie Satie, son of Alfred Satie and Jane Leslie Anton, his wife.

29 August, baptism at the Anglican Church.

1872   9 October, in Paris, death of his mother. Eric and his brother Conrad are taken in by their grandparents in Honfleur and on 4 December receive a Catholic baptism.

1878   14 September, his grandmother dies. Eric returns to Paris to live with his father.

1879   21 January, Alfred Satie marries Eugénie Barnetche, a piano teacher.

4 November, Eric is admitted to the Conservatoire National de Musique et de Déclamation in Paris.

1884   9 September, during a holiday in Honfleur, he composes his first known piece, *Allegro*, for piano.

1886   Eric Satie leaves the Conservatoire in order to volunteer for military service. Shortly afterwards he bares his chest to the icy air of a winter's night so as to contract bronchitis which will enable him to obtain a discharge.

1887   Having changed the spelling of his name to Erik, he publishes his first songs through his father, a music publisher in his spare time, and composes the *Sarabandes*.

In the company of his friend of these years, Patrice Contamine, known as J.P. Contamine de Latour, he becomes a regular visitor to the cabaret Le Chat Noir.

1888   Composes the *Gymnopédies*.

1889   Composes a *Gnossienne*, after hearing 'exotic' music at the Exposition Universelle, at the foot of the newly inaugurated Eiffel Tower, and publishes *Ogives*, modelled on Gregorian music reinterpreted in his own way.

1890   Settles in Montmartre in a small room at 6, rue Cortot.

Takes over the post of conductor of the Chat Noir orchestra from Victor Dynam Fumet.

1891   Meets Claude Achille Debussy and Sâr Péladan, who appoints him 'maître de chapelle de la Rose + Croix'. He lets his hair grow and dresses in a long gown.

1892   19 March, at the Galerie Durand Ruel, the first public performance of his works, at the Soirées Rose + Croix.

At the age of twenty-six, presents his first candidature to the Académie des Beaux Arts.

Spectacular break with Sâr Péladan.

Together with J.P. Contamine de Latour, 'presents' *Uspud* to the Paris Opéra.

1893   Meets Suzanne Valadon, with whom he enters into a brief but passionate relationship, the only publicized love affair in his life.

Makes the acquaintance of the young Ravel, who conceives his first composition under his influence.

15 October, now separated from Valadon, he founds the Eglise Métropolitaine d'Art de Jésus Conducteur, of which he appoints himself 'Parcier and Maître de Chapelle.'

1895   He founds the *Cartulaire*, the journal of his Church, and sends several 'bulls of excommunication' to the best-known artistic and literary personalities of Paris, including the critic Willy, husband of the writer Colette.

He buys seven identical velvet suits which, for seven years, he wears to the exclusion of everything else.

1896   His increasingly disastrous financial situation forces him to leave his modest room for an even smaller room — the 'Cupboard' — at the same address, 6, rue Cortot.

1897   20 February, two *Gymnopédies*, orchestrated by Debussy, are performed at a concert of the very influential Société Nationale at the Salle Erard.

1898   He leaves Montmartre and moves into the Maison des Quatre Cheminées in Arcueil-Cachan. No one ever entered his room there during his lifetime, apart from a few waifs and strays who only stayed for a short time.

1899   Becomes paid accompanist to the cabaret singer Vincent Hyspa.

Composes a few music-hall songs, mostly for Paulette Darty, the 'Queen of the Slow Waltz'.

1900   Now that his ecclesiastical period is over and done with, he composes a *Verset laique & somptueux* for the Exposition Universelle.

1902 The performance of Debussy's *Pelléas et Mélisande*, the product of an aesthetic to whose elaboration he contributed, causes in him a profound crisis.

1903 Composes *Morceaux en forme de poire*.

23 December, death of his father.

1905 At the age of thirty-nine he enrolls in Albert Roussel's course in counterpoint at the Schola Cantorum.

1908 Furnished with a diploma as a contrapuntalist, he participates actively in the social life of the little township of Arcueil-Cachan.

From this time on he adopts the uniform of the minor civil servant: bowler hat, dark jacket, stiff collar and umbrella.

1909 4 July, he is decorated with the 'Palmes Académiques' for services to the community.

As 'superintendent' of the Patronage laïque of Arcueil-Cachan he takes entire classes of children for outings on Thursday afternoons.

1910 Is rediscovered by Ravel as a 'precursor' of Debussy.

Thanks to the support of Ravel and the Jeunes Ravêlites, his works are played at concerts and achieve publication.

Meets Igor Stravinsky at the home of Debussy.

1912 Composes *Aperçus désagréables*, the outcome of his studies at the Schola, with which his young friends disagree.

Meets the great pianist Ricardo Viñes, for whom he composes some sixty short pieces in less than three years. The peak achievement of this period, which he describes himself as 'fantaisiste', is the collection *Sports & Divertissements* (1914).

1914 The outbreak of World War I temporarily halts his productivity, because concert halls and publishing houses close one after the other.

1915 Composes *Cinq Grimaces* for *A Midsummer Night's Dream*, which Varèse plans to produce at the Cirque Médrano. The project is never realized.

1916 Several Montparnasse artists and poets organize concerts, later to be combined with exhibitions of paintings, in a former studio in Montparnasse, the Salle Huyghens. Here Cocteau hears Satie's music for the first time and suggests collaborating with him on a ballet for Diaghilev. Soon afterwards they are joined by Picasso.

1917 8 March, breaks finally with Debussy, who dies the following year.

18 May, the Ballets Russes perform *Parade*, a 'realist' ballet by Satie,

Cocteau and Picasso with choreography by Massine and an introduction by Apollinaire, at the Théâtre du Chatelet. The 'revolutionary' novelty of this production is interpreted by the public and most of the critics as a work of demolition of French values for the benefit of the enemy.

After replying too outspokenly to one critic, and on an open postcard, Satie is taken to court and found guilty of slander.

With a few young musicians who demonstrated in his favour after *Parade*, he forms the group of the Nouveaux Jeunes.

1918   He reads his satirical essay *In Praise of Critics* at the Théâtre du Vieux Colombier.

He composes the 'symphonic drama' *Socrate*, based on Plato's Dialogues, for Princess de Polignac's private receptions.

1920   14 February, the first performance of *Socrate*, is greeted with laughter by the Paris audience, who trust to the composer's reputation as a humorist.

8 March, at the Galerie Barbazanges, he tries out his first Furniture Music, a music 'that is not to be listened to'.

The Group of Six is formed after his aesthetic principles.

Under the title *La Belle Excentrique* he composes for the dancer Caryathis a suite of dances recalling his music-hall years.

1921   Establishes friendship with Brancusi, Léger, Derain, Duchamp and Man Ray.

24 May, Pierre Bertin produces his 'pre-dadaist' piece *Le Piège de Méduse* (written in 1913) at the Théâtre Michel.

D.H. Kahnweiler publishes this piece in a bibliophile edition that contains Braque's first works as an illustrator.

1922   Takes sides with Tzara in his dispute with André Breton over the Congress of Paris.

1923   Composes a 'divertissement', *La Statue retrouvée*, for Count Etienne de Beaumont's masked ball on the theme of antiquities in the era of Louis XIV, with costumes by Picasso and Jean Hugo and choreography by Massine.

He takes part, alongside Tristan Tzara, in the Soirée du Coeur à Barbe, the last Dadaist manifestation in Paris, which ended with a memorable brawl instigated by Breton and his friends.

The Ecole d'Arcueil is formed after his aesthetic principles.

1924 In collaboration with Picasso and Massine composes *Mercure*, 'poses plastiques', which is produced on 16 June at the Théâtre de la Cigale as part of Count Etienne de Beaumont's Soirée de Paris.

In collaboration with the painter Picabia, the filmmaker René Clair and the choreographer Jean Börlin, composes the ballet 'instantanéiste' *Relâche*, with a 'cinematographic interlude', which was performed on 4 December by the Ballets Suédois at the Théâtre des Champs Elysées.

1925 Satie, who has been suffering for some time from cirrhosis of the liver, develops double pneumonia and is admitted, on 15 February, to the Saint Joseph Hospital, where he dies on 1 July in extreme poverty.

He receives a religious funeral at Arcueil.

His friends enter his room for the first time. It looks to them like a combination of Aladin's cave and a spider's web.

ORIGIN OF LETTERS
FROM SATIE

to the Académie des Beaux Arts	June 1892; Institut de France Archives
to Georges Auric	[December 1913]; excerpt published in G.A., *Quand j'étais là*, Paris: Grasset, 1979, page 21
to Edith de Beaumont	4 April, 1919; Private Collection 11 April, 1919; Idem 23 March, 1922; Idem 26 December, 1922; Idem 31 December, 1922; Idem 22 March, 1923; Idem 14 May, 1923; Idem
to Etienne de Beaumont	24 August, 1918; Idem 27 April, 1923; Idem 10 May, 1924; Idem
to Pierre Bertin	[November 1918]; Idem 26 June, 1919; Idem 1 March, 1920; Idem
to Monsieur Bertrand	[November 1892]; excerpt published in J.P. Contamine de Latour, *Erik Satie intime*, in *Comoedia*, 6 August, 1925, page 3 [December 1892]; Idem
to Constantin Brancusi	16 April, 1923: Bibliothèque Litt. Jacques Doucet, Brancusi Archives
to Caryathis	[June 1921; excerpt published in Elise Jouhandeau, *Joies et Douleurs d'une Belle Excentrique*, Vol. III, 'Le Spleen empanaché', page 144
to the Catholic Artists and to all the Christians	15 October, 1893; published in *Le Coeur*, Vol. I, n. 6–7, September–October 1893, 'Littérature' column
to Countess de Chabannes	3 June, 1914; Private Collection
to René Chalupt	[1919]; excerpt published in René Chalupt, *Quelques souvenirs sur Erik Satie*, in *La Revue musicale*, no 214, special issue 'Erik Satie, son temps et ses amis', June 1952, page 45
to René Clair	23 October, 1924; Private Collection
to Jean Cocteau	[25 April, 1916]; Idem [2 May, 1916]; Idem

	8 June, 1916; Idem 19 October, 1916; Idem
to Paul Collaer	16 May, 1920; Idem 18 October, 1924; Idem 27 October, 1924; Idem
to *Comoedia*	13 February, 1922 [signed by Eluard, Ribemont-Dessaignes and Tzara too]; published in *Comoedia*, 14 February, 1922
to the Conservatoire National de Musique et de Déclamation	17 November, 1892; Private Collection, included in the manuscript of *Uspud*
to J.P. Contamine de Latour	17 November, 1892; Idem
to Paulette Darty	6 January, 1907; Private Collection
to Claude Debussy	17 August, 1903; published in *Trois Lettres d'Erik Satie à Claude Debussy (1903)* edited by Henri Bourgeaud, *Revue de Musicologie*, 1962, special issue 'Claude Debussy 1862–1962', pages 70–73
to Emma Debussy	8 March, 1917; published in *Debussy e il Simbolismo* by Guy Cogeval and François Lesure, Rome: Fratelli Palombi, 1984, p. 149
to Roger Désormière	11 May, 1924; Private Collection
to Serge de Diaghilev	19 June, 1923; Bibliothèque de l'Opéra de Paris, Boris Kochno Collection
to Louis Durey	1 November, 1918; Private Collection
to Misia Edwards	15 May, 1916; Idem 9 July, 1916; Idem [the same modified, in Misia Sert, *Misia*, Paris, Gallimard, 1952, page 117]
to Germaine Everling	27 August, 1924; Bibliothèque litt. Jacques Doucet, Picabia Archives
to Gaultier Garguille	14 August, 1892; published in Gaultier Garguille, *Propos de coulisses*, in *Gil Blas*, XIV, no 4655, 16 August, 1892
to Henry Gauthier Villars	2 May, 1895, published in *Cartulaire*, n.1-63, May 1895 14 May, 1895; Idem
to Valentine Gross	25 April, 1916; formerly in the Valentine Hugo Collection, transcribed by Jean Roy 13 July, 1916; Idem 8 August, 1916; Idem 10 August, 1916; reproduced in *Souvenir de Parade*, painting-collage by Valentine Hugo, 1965. Foundation Erik Satie Collection 24 August, 1916; published in Douglas Cooper, *Picasso Théâtre*, Paris:

Cercle d'Art, 1967, page 17

1 September, 1916; formerly in the Valentine Hugo Collection, transcribed by Jean Roy

14 September, 1916; reproduced in facsimile in Douglas Cooper, op.cit., page 340

20 September, 1916; Idem, page 341

2 December, 1916; formerly in the Valentine Hugo Collection, transcribed by Jean Roy

2 January, 1917; Idem

6 January, 1917; reproduced in facsimile in *La Revue Musicale*, n.214, special issue: 'Erik Satie, son Temps et ses Amis', June 1952

18 January, 1917; Idem

13 December, 1920; published in Douglas Cooper, op.cit., page 17

to Reynaldo Hahn	1893; published in R. Hahn, *Chronique musicale*, in *Le Figaro*, 9 December, 1937
to Vincent Hyspa	22 October, 1909; published in Théophile Briant, *Hyspa et Satie*, in *Le Goéland*, Vol. 1, n.11, 22 April, 1937
to Vincent d'Indy	[September 1905]; draft copy, Bibliothèque Nationale, Music Department, Satie Manuscripts
to *Intermédiaire des Chercheurs et des Curieux*	[1896?]; published, under the pseudonym of 'César Birotteau', in *L'Intermédiaire des Chercheurs et des Curieux*, [1896?]
to Maxime Benjamin Jacob	21 April, 1923; Private Collection
to George Jean-Aubry	19 November, 1919; Private Collection, transcribed by Thierry Bodin
to Charles Koechlin	28 September, 1918; Private Collection 6 February, 1924; Idem
to Ernest Legrand	18 December, 1892; Private Collection Nineties; Private Collection, included in the manuscript of *Uspud*
to Aurélien Lugné Poe	24 January, 1895; published in Erik Satie, *Commune qui mundi nefas*, [Paris, Librairie de l'Art Indépendant, 1895]
to Rolf de Maré	12 October, 1923; published in *L'Echo des Champs Elysées*, 15 October 1923 23 November, 1923; Dansmuseet, Ballets Suédois Archives 2 April, 1924; Idem 29 June, 1924; Idem 10 January, 1925; Idem

to Léonide Massine	7 April, 1924; Private Collection 15 April, 1924; Idem 4 May, 1924; Idem
to Pierre de Massot	18 March, 1924; Idem 27 July, 1924; Idem
to Wieland Mayr	21 June, 1924; Idem
to Victor Emile Michelet	23 November, 1924; the Library of Congress, Music Division
to Darius Milhaud	5 March, 1920; Private Collection 16 June, 1924; Idem 10 August, 1924; Idem
to Francis Picabia	3 January, 1921; Bibliothèque Litt. Jacques Doucet, Picabia Archives 30 January, 1921; Idem 8 February, 1924; Idem
to Jean Poueigh	30 May, 1917; Préfecture de Police de Paris Archives excerpts transcribed in the records of the trial of First Instance Poueigh against Satie, 12 July, 1917 3 June, 1917; Idem 5 June, 1917; Idem [10 September, 1917]; draft copy, Bibliothèque Nationale Music Department, Satie Manuscripts
to Francis Poulenc	[October 1915]; published in *Quelques Opinions de Musiciens sur César Franck*, in *La Revue musicale*, Vol. II, N.1, 1 November, 1921 29 September, 1917; published in Francis Poulenc, *Correspondance, 1915–1963*, edited by Hélène de Wendel, Paris: Editions du Seuil, 1967, page 14
to Henry Prunières	14 September, 1917; Private Collection 3 April, 1918; Idem
to Marcel Raval	21 October, 1924; Idem
to Maurice Ravel	4 March, 1911; Bibliothèque Nationale, Music Department, Satie Autograph Letters
to Roland Manuel	26 October, 1913; Private Collection 19 April, 1916; Idem August 1917; Idem 14 March, 1918; Idem
to Albert Roussel	6 October, 1907; Private Collection
to Camille Saint Saëns	17 May, 1894; published in *Le Menestrel*, LX, n.2314, 10 June, 1894

to Conrad Satie   28 June, 1893; formerly in the Conrad Satie Collection, transcribed by P.D. Templier
[12 July, 1896?]; Idem
9 October, 1898; Idem
8 November, 1898; Idem
21 November, 1898; Idem
22 January, 1899; Idem
5 February, 1899; Idem
14 March, 1899; Idem
[3 April, 1899]; Idem
14 April, 1899; published facsimile in P.D. Templier, *Erik Satie*, Paris: Rieder, 1932, plate XXVI
15 May, 1899; formerly in the Conrad Satie Collection, transcribed by P.D. Templier
4 July, 1899; Idem
22 July, 1899; Idem
December 1899; Idem
7 June, 1900; Idem
June 1901; Idem
23 February, 1901; Idem
14 January, 1911; reproduced in facsimile in P.D. Templier, op.cit., plate XXXIII, n.1
17 January, 1911; formerly in the Conrad Satie Collection, transcribed by P.D. Templier
27 March, 1911; Idem
11 April, 1911; Idem

to Erik Satie   20 February, 1889; published, under the pseudonym of 'Femme Lengrenage', in *La Lanterne Japonaise*, Vol II, No 15, 23 March, 1889
24 July, 1896; Private Collection

to Henri Sauguet   7 February, 1924; Idem

to Igor Stravinsky   3 July, 1922; published in *Avec Stravinsky*, Monaco: Editions du Rocher, 1958, page 206
9 August, 1922; Idem, page 207
15 September, 1923; Idem, page 208 [facsimilé]

to Pierre Alexandre Templier   13 September, 1909; Fondation Erik Satie Archives

to Mrs G.M. Tuttle   5 November, 1918; Private Collection

to Tristan Tzara   29 June, 1923; Bibliothèque Litt. Jacques Doucet, Tristan Tzara Archives
7 July, 1923; Ibidem

to Suzanne Valadon	11 March, 1893; Musée National d'Art Moderne, Documentation Department, Robert Le Masle Collection
to Edgard Varèse	6 February, 1916; Private Collection
to Léon Louis Veyssière	8 January, 1921; Idem
to Louis Grégoire Veyssière	14 August, 1910; published in *L'Avenir d'Arcueil-Cachan*, Vol. III, n.72, 4 September, 1910
to Ricardo Viñes	30 March, 1912; formerly in the Ricardo Viñes Collection, transcribed by Hernando Viñes 19 April, 1916; Private Collection, transcribed by Thierry Bodin [July 1917]; excerpt published in catalogue Charavay, November 1950 [July 1917?]; formerly in the R. Viñes Collection, transcribed by Hernando Viñes

ORIGIN OF LETTERS TO SATIE

from J.P. Contamine de Latour	17 November, 1892; Private Collection, included in the manuscript of *Uspud*
from Charles Koechlin	30 September, [1918]; Private Collection

ORIGIN OF LETTERS ABOUT SATIE

Guillaume Apollinaire to Misia Edwards	13 July, 1917; Private Collection
to Maître José Théry	24 June, [1917]; Idem
André Breton to Francis Picabia	15 February, 1922; published in Michel Sanouillet, *Dada à Paris*, Paris: J.J. Pauvest, 1965, p. 515
Jean Cocteau to Misia Edwards	[June 1916]; published from a draft copy found in the V. Hugo Collection, in Francis Steegmuller, *Cocteau*, Paris: Buchet Chastel, 1973, p. 117–118 June–July 1916; published in Misia Sert, *Misia*, op. cit., p. 142

	June 1916; Private Collection
	10 October, 1916; Idem
	[13 July, 1917]; Idem
to Valentine Gross	1 May, [1916]; published in Anne de Margerie, *Valentine Hugo*, Paris: Jacques Damase, 1983, page 123
	[3 May, 1916]; formerly in the Valentine Hugo Collection, transcribed by A. de Margerie
	[May 1916]; Idem
	13 July, 1916; excerpt published in F. Steegmuller, op. cit., p. 124
	5 August, 1916; published in A. de Margerie, op. cit., page 124
	9 August, 1916; excerpt published in F. Steegmuller, op. cit., p. 124
	12 August, 1916; published in A. de Margerie, op. cit., p. 125
	31 August, 1916; excerpt published in F. Steegmuller, op. cit., p. 125
	4 September, 1916, published in A. de Margerie, op. cit., p. 126
	22 September, 1916; formerly in the V. Hugo Collection, transcribed by A. de Margerie
	11 February, 1917; published in F. Steegmuller, op. cit., p. 132
	16 February, 1917; Idem
Claude Debussy to Jacques Durand	8 August, 1914; published in Claude Debussy, *Lettres, 1884–1918*, edited by François Lesure, Paris: Hermann, 1980, page 257
to Francisco Lacerda	5 September, 1908; Idem, pages 173–174.
Max Jacob to Jacques Doucet	10 August, 1917; Bibliothèque Litt. Jacques Doucet, Jacques Doucet Archives
Ernest Legrand to an unidentified correspondent	22 May, 1934; Private Collection, included in the manuscript of *Uspud*
Raymonde Linossier to Francis Poulenc	[6 July, 1925]: Private Collection
Léonide Massine to Jean Cocteau	27 January, 1917: Idem
Pierre de Massot to Francis Picabia	22 January, 1924: Bibliothèque Litt. Jacques Doucet, Picabia Archives
	26 January, 1924: Idem
	3 February, 1924: Idem
	16 June 1924: Idem
	19 June, 1925: Idem
Emile Pessard to an unidentified Academician	[June 1892]: Private Collection

Francis Picabia to André Breton	17 February, 1922; Bibliothèque Nationale Manuscripts Department, Dossier 'Congrès de Paris'
to Tristan Tzara	28 March, 1919; Bibliothèque Litt. Jacques Doucet, Tzara Archives
Pablo Picasso to Jean Cocteau	1 February, 1917; reproduced in facsimile in Douglas Cooper, op.cit., page 329
Francis Poulenc to Ricardo Viñes	26 September, 1917; published in Francis Poulenc, op. cit., p. 13–14
Alfred Satie to Albert Sorel	25 March, 1865; Private Collection
Suzanne Valadon to Conrad Satie	[Summer 1926]; Bibliothèque Nationale, Music Department, Autograph Letters

BIBLIOGRAPHY

BOOKS

Bain, Robert — *The Clans and Tartans of Scotland*, Glasgow and London: Fontana-Collins, 1968

Beach, Sylvia — *Shakespeare & Co*, London: Faber and Faber, 1960

Baltrušaitis, Jurgis — *La Quête d'Isis*, Paris: Olivier Perrin, 1967

Cendrars, Blaise — *Feuilles de route*, Paris: Au Sans Pareil, 1924
Blaise Cendrars vous parle, by Michel Manoll et Albert Riéra, Paris: Denoël, 1952

Cocteau, Jean — *Picasso*, Paris: Stock, 1924
Maalesh, Journal d'une tournée de théâtre, Paris: Gallimard, 1949

Curnonsky — *Le Voyage de M. Dortigois*, Paris, 1919

Everling, Germaine — *L'Anneau de Saturne*, Paris: Fayard, 1960

Gide, André — *Journal 1889–1939*, Paris: Gallimard, Pléïade, 1948

Grand Carteret, John — *Raphaël et Gambrinus ou l'art dans la brasserie*, Paris: Louis Westhausser, 1886

Hoérée, Arthur — *Albert Roussel*, Paris: Rieder, 1938

Huelsenbeck, Richard — *Almanach Dada*, Berlin: Erich Reiss, 1920

Josephson, Matthew — *My Life among the Surrealists*, New York: Holt, Reinhart & Winston, 1962

Jouhandeau, Elise — *Joies et Douleurs d'une Belle Excentrique*, t. 111, *Le Spleen empanaché*, Paris: Flammarion, 1960

Laloy, Louis — *La Musique retrouvée (1902–1927)*, Paris: Plon, 1928

Man Ray — *Self portrait*, London: André Deutsch, 1963

Maritain, Jacques — *Reponse à Jean Cocteau*, Paris: Librairie Stock, 1926

Milhaud, Darius — *Notes sans musique*, Paris: René Julliard, 1949

Morand, Paul — *Journal d'un Attaché d'Ambassade, 1916–1917*, Paris: Gallimard, 1963

Pougy, Liane de — *Mes Cahiers bleus*, Paris: Librairie Plon, 1977

Radiguet, Raymond — *Le Bal du Comte d'Orgel*, Paris: Grasset, 1924
London: Marion Boyars 1968,

Rusiñol, Santiago — *Impresiones de Arte*, Barcelona, 1897

Satie, Erik	*Ecrits*, edited by Ornella Volta, Paris: Champ libre, 1977
Stravinsky, Igor	*An Autobiography*, New York: Simon & Schuster, 1936 and London: Marion Boyars, 1975
Stein, Gertrude	*The Autobiography of Alice Toklas*, New York: Harcourt Brace, 1933
Stravinsky Igor and Robert Craft	*Memories and Commentaries*, London: Faber and Faber, 1959
Tzara, Tristan	*Oeuvres complètes* I, edited by Henri Béhar, Paris: Flammarion, 1975

NEWSPAPERS, REVIEWS

Approdo musicale, L'	no. 19–20, 1965. Paul Collaer, *Il Gruppo dei Sei*
Annales, Les	LVIII, n.4, 1951 Pierre Bertin, *Erik Satie et le Groupe des Six*
Cahiers Dada-Surréalisme	no. 1, 1966 Pierre de Massot, *Edgar Varèse*
Comœdia	no. 5, 6, 8 August, 1925 J.P. Contamine de Latour, *Erik Satie intime; Souvenirs de Jeunesse*
Danse, La	November–December, 1924 issue devoted to the 'Ballets Suédois'
Excelsior, L'	11 May, 1917 Guillaume Apollinaire, *Parade et l'Esprit Nouveau*
Figaro, Le	9 December, 1937 Reynaldo Hahn, *Chronique musicale. Le Rideau de Paris: l'Humeur d'Erik Satie*
Lui	no. 123, April 1974 *Entretien avec Louis Aragon*
Perspectives of New Music	111, no. 2, Spring–Summer 1965 Gunther Schuller, *Conversation with Varèse*
Sept Arts	no. 9, 1 January 1925 Fernand Léger, *Relâche*

UNPUBLISHED TEXTS

Darty, Paulette — *Ma première rencontre avec Satie*, c. 1928. Private collection.

Grass-Mick, Augustin — *Souvenirs autour d'Erik Satie*, c. 1950. Idem.

Hugo, Jean — Correspondence with the author. Idem.

Satie, Conrad — Note-book, 1914–1925. Idem.

Veyssière, Léon-Louis — *Souvenirs et Réflexions sur Erik Satie*, c. 1950. Idem.

BOOKS ON ERIK SATIE IN ENGLISH

Templier, Pierre-Daniel — *Erik Satie* [1932], translated from french by Elena L. French and David S. French, Cambridge, Massachusetts: MIT Press, 1969; New York, Dover, 1980.

Myers, Rollo — *Erik Satie*, London: Denis Dobson, 1948; New York: Dover, 1968

Harding, James — *Erik Satie*, London: Secker & Warburg, 1975

Gillmor, Alan M. — *Erik Satie*, Boston: Twayne Publ., div. of G.K. Hall & Co., 1988

INDEX

Page numbers in italics refer to portraits

DATE DUE

4/29/04			
MAY 0 4 2004			